Praise for *The Way*

"Jeremy and Ally Butrous have written a very practical, helpful, insightful book dealing with a broad understanding of prosperity that goes beyond financial prosperity to include prosperity in all areas of life. I recommend it to all, especially those beginning their families and careers, though it will benefit all age groups. This book contains divine wisdom."

—RANDY CLARK, DD, DMIN, THD, MDIV, BS, PRESIDENT OF GLOBAL
AWAKENING THEOLOGICAL SEMINARY, GLOBALAWAKENING.COM

"As it pertains to God's definition of prosperity, I believe financial prosperity is the least of His concerns. I say this because if a believer doesn't first prosper in their character and inner life, financial prosperity has the potential to cause severe devastation in every other area of life. You can trust these words because I have firsthand experience with this. *The Ways of Prosperity* is an important book for our generation—a generation that desperately needs to learn the true meaning of divine prosperity."

—BRIAN "HEAD" WELCH, COFOUNDER OF THE GRAMMY AWARD–WINNING
BAND KORN; *NEW YORK TIMES* BESTSELLING AUTHOR, *SAVE ME FROM MYSELF*;
AND COSTAR OF THE SHOWTIME DOCUMENTARY *LOUD KRAZY LOVE*

"Ally and Jeremy empower you with forty-nine ways to increase prosperity in seven areas of your life. They provide direction and vision, helping you identify ways to upgrade your life and reach your greatest potential."

—JON GORDON, BESTSELLING AUTHOR OF *THE CARPENTER AND THE SEED*

"The Christian vision and reality of a flourishing and prosperous life is holistic, encompassing every facet of one's life. What I appreciate most about *The Ways of Prosperity* is its keeping of this holistic perspective, all while remaining grounded in Scripture and faith. Jeremy and Ally speak from their hearts as well as from their own life stories, and I believe that these insights collected here have capacity to speak into yours as well."

—DAVID C. WANG, THM, PHD, ASSOCIATE PROFESSOR OF PSYCHOLOGY,
ROSEMEAD SCHOOL OF PSYCHOLOGY, BIOLA UNIVERSITY

"Jeremy and his wife, Ally Butrous, have written a beautiful book that breaks down a complex and misunderstood topic: prosperity. This book has redefined prosperity and will set the readers free to understand the favor God has for them and will nourish their souls as they begin to live in God's ways of prosperity."

—BOB HASSON, CEO OF R.M. HASSON PAINTING
CONTRACTORS, INC.; AUTHOR OF *THE BUSINESS OF HONOR*

"This book is the most comprehensive and holistic book I have read on true prosperity. It goes deep and practical and is equal parts revelation and wisdom. I want to highly recommend *The Ways of Prosperity* which really did pleasantly surprise me and even challenged me in such a positive way."

—JOHNNY ENLOW, INTERNATIONAL SPEAKER; AUTHOR, *THE SEVEN MOUNTAIN PROPHECY*; CO-SENIOR PASTOR, DAYSTAR CHURCH, ATLANTA, GEORGIA; COFOUNDER, RESTORE7 MINISTRY

The Ways of Prosperity

God's Provision for Every Area of Your Life

JEREMY BUTROUS
ALLY BUTROUS

EMANATE
BOOKS

Published in Nashville, Tennessee, by Emanate Books, an imprint of Thomas Nelson. Emanate Books and Thomas Nelson are registered trademarks of HarperCollins Christian Publishing, Inc.

Thomas Nelson titles may be purchased in bulk for educational, business, fund-raising, or sales promotional use. For information, please e-mail SpecialMarkets@ThomasNelson.com.

Unless otherwise noted, Scripture quotations are taken from New American Standard Bible®. Copyright © 1960, 1962, 1963, 1968, 1971, 1972, 1973, 1975, 1977, 1995 by The Lockman Foundation. Used by permission. (www.Lockman.org) Scripture quotations marked AMP are from the Amplified® Bible. Copyright © 1954, 1958, 1962, 1964, 1965, 1987 by The Lockman Foundation. Used by permission. (www.Lockman.org) Scripture quotations marked BSB are from The Holy Bible, Berean Study Bible, BSB. Copyright ©2016, 2018 by Bible Hub. Used by Permission. All Rights Reserved Worldwide. Scripture quotations marked ESV are from the ESV® Bible (The Holy Bible, English Standard Version®). Copyright © 2001 by Crossway, a publishing ministry of Good News Publishers. Used by permission. All rights reserved. Scripture quotations marked HCSB are from the Holman Christian Standard Bible®. Copyright © 1999, 2000, 2002, 2003, 2009 by Holman Bible Publishers. Used by permission. HCSB® is a federally registered trademark of Holman Bible Publishers. Scripture quotations marked KJV are from the King James Bible. Public domain. Scripture quotations marked NIV are from the Holy Bible, New International Version®, NIV®. Copyright © 1973, 1978, 1984, 2011 by Biblica, Inc.® Used by permission of Zondervan. All rights reserved worldwide. www.Zondervan.com. The "NIV" and "New International Version" are trademarks registered in the United States Patent and Trademark Office by Biblica, Inc.® Scripture quotations marked NKJV are from the New King James Version®. © 1982 by Thomas Nelson. Used by permission. All rights reserved. Scripture quotations marked NLT are from the Holy Bible, New Living Translation. © 1996, 2004, 2007, 2013, 2015 by Tyndale House Foundation. Used by permission of Tyndale House Publishers, Inc., Carol Stream, Illinois 60188. All rights reserved. Scripture quotations marked NRSV are from New Revised Standard Version Bible. Copyright © 1989 National Council of the Churches of Christ in the United States of America. Used by permission. All rights reserved. Scripture quotations marked TLB are from The Living Bible. Copyright © 1971. Used by permission of Tyndale House Publishers, Inc., Carol Stream, Illinois 60188. All rights reserved.

Any Internet addresses, phone numbers, or company or product information printed in this book are offered as a resource and are not intended in any way to be or to imply an endorsement by Thomas Nelson, nor does Thomas Nelson vouch for the existence, content, or services of these sites, phone numbers, companies, or products beyond the life of this book.

ISBN 978-0-7852-3425-8 (eBook)
ISBN 978-0-7852-3424-1 (TP)

Library of Congress Control Number: 2020939125

Printed in the United States of America
20 21 22 23 24 LSC 10 9 8 7 6 5 4 3 2 1

Contents

PART 5: INCREASING PROFESSIONAL PROSPERITY

PART 6: INCREASING MINDSETS THAT CREATE PROSPERITY

PART 7: INCREASING SOCIAL PROSPERITY

Introduction

YOUR INVITATION TO A LIFE OF PROSPERITY

What if you were immersed in a daily experience of prosperity? An experience in which you started to powerfully live out John's prayer: "Beloved, I pray that you may prosper in all things and be in health, just as your soul prospers" (3 John 1:2 NKJV)? Imagine your prosperity experienced on a soul level. You find yourself on a one-way conveyor belt on a journey that would reveal daily hope and impact all your life. What would happen next?

It is likely that your spiritual life would bloom as never before. You would have a sound mind. Your relationships would be empowering and fulfilling. Your work would be more productive and enriching. Your emotional life would be filled with peace and hope. Your community would flourish and start brimming with life. Your finances would tell a story of the goodness of God. Imagine how all of life would start to change and echo of heaven's prosperity, vision, and love. Think about how you might be better equipped to walk out your kingdom calling completely. This was the very invitation that we were given years ago. This was the invitation that led us to write this book.

At the time we received this invitation, I (Ally) was working in the field of psychology, helping people learn to thrive. I (Jeremy) had finished the school of ministry and had been ghostwriting Christian books with an interest in theology. I was also working with several notable Christian authors and speakers. Our evening conversations became filled with thoughts about prosperity from both a psychological and theological perspective. It was quite literally a marriage of the two. Initially, all we knew was that the prosperity God called us to was not centered around finances. In fact, living in Los Angeles, it was easy to identify people who had money yet did not seem to be prospering in any other aspect of their lives.

We believe it is time for the misleading and limiting "prosperity gospel" message to be abolished. True prosperity is so much more. In essence it is a life in which we partner with Jesus. It is journeying with Him in intimate, loving, powerful, and purposeful ways. In this context, money is viewed simply as a tool to maximize our opportunity to display the will of the Father.

Sadly, tradition and culture have presented us with a minimalist perspective on the ways God wants to prosper us. It is easy for us to miss the depth of God's goodness in all the facets and avenues of His love. God wants to be our ultimate provider. He wants us to partner with the supernatural and natural ways of provision. Larry Randolph, from Living Rain Ministries, said, "God is an instant miracle worker, but His nature is that of a farmer."[1] Through the message of this book, we hope you will learn how to become a participant in this miraculous process.

This is your invitation to live your most prosperous life. We want to invite you to discover the upgrades God has hidden for you—mysteries stored up for you from before time began. Through this process, God will be more deeply revealed as the ultimate life source of good, the ultimate provider, the ultimate King. This book was created to help you become aware of the ways God originally designed you to receive His blessings. Our Father longs to bring us the healthiest perspective on provision so we can truly say we live the abundant life Jesus died to give us. Ally and I want to take you to the start of our prosperity journey—a journey we believe began in insight from biblical times. Our journey starts with stories and understanding from the Bible.

Imagine with us for a moment that one night you go to bed, just like any other night, but you have a vivid and powerful dream. In this dream you become immersed in the middle of a story, as if you were there in real time, watching it all unfold. You see the Sea of Tiberias and seven tired and discouraged men fishing in a boat. You smell the early morning air and see the pink color that indicates the sun is about to rise. You smell the salty seawater; you hear water lapping against the boat.

You look to the shore. There is one man walking alone on the shore. He turns to the boat and asks, "Children, do you have any fish?" The men, maybe in a bit of a frustrated tone, shout back no!

The man on the shore responds, "Cast the net on the right side of the boat, and you will find some." The men grumble but do what he said.

Suddenly, you hear fish flapping around in the water, trying to get free of the net. You can smell the fish and hear the men full of surprise, joy, and hope as they yell to one another and try to stabilize the boat, which can barely hold such a catch. You wonder why the fish did not just jump in the boat; the man on shore is so powerful, he probably could have caused that to happen. Instead, the men had to work hard to receive what was freely given. They used their natural skills as fishermen, natural physical strength, and natural wisdom to partner with heavenly provision. This partnership put them in the midst of a very prosperous situation. Perhaps it was the most prosperous moment in their fishing careers. (Story can be found in John 21 ESV.)

Though you are dreaming, you recognize the symbolism here. Matthew 13:47 says, "Again, the kingdom of heaven is like a dragnet cast into the sea, and gathering fish of every kind." In this passage Jesus went on to say that the fish were sorted and the bad ones thrown out. It is like this with prosperity. We need to look diligently at the natural ways of provision that are given, to find out what is from God and what is not. One way we do that throughout this book is drawing on concepts discussed in the social sciences.

Many think the kingdom of heaven is a place where we will go one day, but in Luke 17:21, Jesus says, "The kingdom of God is within you" (NKJV). And Romans 14:17 says, "For the Kingdom of God is . . . living a life of goodness and peace and joy in the Holy Spirit" (NLT). Finally, the kingdom of God is described as inner prosperity of emotions, thoughts, and relationships.

As these verses come to mind, you see the men jump out of the boat and walk to the dry sand. They count out 153 fish. And then the moment happens: they realize the man on shore, the one bringing all this prosperity, is Jesus. He is the provider of their financially prosperous catch. But He is much more than that.

In one sobering moment, they realize He is the waymaker for their abundant emotional healing and health after they feared He had died and they were heartbroken, feeling all was lost. He gave them information about who He was and who they were to help renew their minds and thoughts about God, their lives, and their futures. He shared with them Himself, the one and only way for them to be spiritually restored to God the Father for eternity. He provided them with their life mission, calling, identity, and work. He gave them the ability to build a prosperous church community. He provided understanding for how to create prosperous relationships.

Now, imagine you've had this dream and you wake up in the early morning before dawn. As the dream is fading, you hear a voice. You're not absolutely sure if it is from the world of the dream or the world of the waking. The voice says, "There are 153 ways to My prosperity. Do you want to know what they are?"

This was the very dream and experience I (Jeremy) had years ago. It birthed a journey to pursue with Ally this revelation about the true nature of prosperity. As our lives started more fully prospering, we began to sense a burning desire to share these ways of prosperity with others. Proverbs 25:2 says, "It is God's privilege to conceal things and the king's privilege to discover them" (NLT). As heirs with Christ, it was our privilege to discover many ways of prosperity that God had concealed as treasures in His Word. It is our privilege now to help you discover all the ways of prosperity.

How many ways of prosperity are you walking in? The disciples' net was worth more than the fish it contained or the money the fish could bring. That net brought them back safely to shore to connect with Jesus and start to prosper in countless ways. Have you fully explored what Jesus has given you to help you prosper? What is your relational, spiritual, emotional, professional, and financial net worth? What mysteries about how you can more fully prosper through Jesus have been hidden for you to discover through this book and the Word of God?

After God invited me to know the ways of prosperity, during the next hour the Holy Spirit brought to mind verses that revealed how the Bible confirms this holistic view of prosperity. Later, the Holy Spirit showed both of us how these ways apply to seven areas of life: relational, spiritual, emotional and physical, financial, professional, mindset, and social. We believe this was a revelation that came from Jesus as an invitation for all of us to live the abundant life His death and resurrection promise.

HOW TO USE THIS BOOK TO INCREASE YOUR PROSPERITY

This book has been written to help you understand the full breadth and scope of the invitation you have to greater prosperity. We believe it will inspire, encourage, and empower you. The concepts, ideas, and activities suggested undergird the journey we have been walking in for years. We believe everyone has a prosperity potential that is great, but only a few people are actively walking it out and partnering with it. Some may be filling only a fraction of their prosperity potential.

A further goal of this book is to help you apply the ways of prosperity to your daily life as a holistic experience. There are seven parts to this book, each part representing one of the seven areas of life and containing seven ways of prosperity—forty-nine in total. It is designed to give you a logical and convenient way to experience a selection of the 153 ways of prosperity—perhaps exploring one a day for seven weeks or one a week for forty-nine weeks.

God is so holistically minded that if we take any one of these forty-nine ways of prosperity, we can apply it to any of the seven areas of life to find prosperity there also. Being slow to anger, for example, increases the prosperity in our relationships, our spiritual walk, our physical and emotional health, and so on.

We all learn in different ways and at different speeds. So, Ally and I felt it would be beneficial to have several components to each way of prosperity for you to consider and interact with:

1. Scripture to help frame what God says about that particular way of prosperity, and in some cases this is the main verse discussing it in the Bible.

2. A short teaching where we share experiences, thoughts, and stories about this way of prosperity applied in the area of life under consideration.

3. A section about *"building* your prosperous life," helping us to live out what we have learned not just with words but in action and truth—actively partnering with the prosperity Jesus has made available.

4. A "prosperity prayer" to directly connect to the heart of God in this way of prosperity. This is not meant to be an all-encompassing prayer but just a place to start, then adding your own prayer.

5. Finally, we encourage you toward continued growth by showing you how you can "create holistic prosperity." We provide one or two sentences for how the current way of prosperity is applied to each area of life. Our hope is that this is just a jump start for you to think, pray, talk, and imagine what could change in each area by applying each way of prosperity.

An important component of this book is that every area is connected. Our spiritual walk impacts our emotions and thoughts. Our relationships impact our social lives and our professions. Our thoughts impact our relationships and how we manage our finances.

Our prayer is that this book becomes a transformative experience of God's love and provision in your life—that you will abundantly prosper as you get to know God's provision and accept your calling to partner with it. Both of us have been walking out and refining these ways for several years. We have truly seen our prosperity grow exponentially and explosively in every area of our lives as we've partnered with God. We know it works. We hope you are ready to increase your prosperity potential today!

PART 1

Increasing Relational Prosperity

Relationships are the conduit to every good thing in life, and no one is better at relationships than God. Jesus is the most relatable person on the planet. In Him everyone can find themselves no matter the situation or season.

God wants all our relationships to thrive. We can begin by learning about relationships based on a biblical foundation coupled with practical stories and research-based tools. Biblically based, holistic prosperity is grounded in relationships, and we have been given the ways of prosperity as our guide and opportunity. We can craft successful relationships when we partner with God's fresh perspective and the ways He provides. Relational prosperity will allow our love to abound, our connections to grow, and our communication to be clear.

1

Building

For he said to Judah, "Let us build these cities and surround them with walls and towers, gates and bars. The land is still ours because we have sought the LORD our God; we have sought Him, and He has given us rest on every side." So they built and prospered.

–2 CHRONICLES 14:7

*H*ave you ever traveled to palaces and churches that showcased the prosperity of their day? It is breathtaking to see what we can build when we set our heart to it! Imagine now that, instead of building the pyramids or the Palace of Versailles in all its splendor, we build our relationships to their full potential.

Building has always been a catalyst for showing off prosperity. How about considering building as a way to get us to prosperity? In 2 Chronicles, Judah's prosperity came while the people were building. Let us consider how the building of cities, walls, and towers are an example for building our relationships and families. We can build highways of communication, monuments of experience, and bridges of love.

I (Jeremy) have been actively building a relationship with my brother Nick for as long as I can remember. One of the ways we build up our relationship is through quality time. Whenever I am on the phone with Nick, we plan times to visit or travel together. In the midst of building time together, we plan and strategize all the projects and things we could do. Our intentionality during those moments carries us through until the next time.

The Bible says that without vision, people perish (Proverbs 29:18). This is also true for relationships. Relationships need a clear plan, like the blueprints for a house. Brick by brick, line upon line, one decision after another, we can deploy building in our communication, experiences, and love. Our daily exchanges with one another are like building cities unto God—beautifully constructed masterpieces that will not be impacted by a passing threat.

God is a master builder and architect. Even His Son Jesus picked up the family business and became a carpenter while on earth. The act of building is definitely on His mind. Just as Jesus would build something out of wood in the natural world, God has given us the ability to build relationally with others spiritually, emotionally, and intellectually. We do so with each action, word, and gesture.

Our relational success is most evident when we make more relational deposits than withdrawals. When we are present and active in the short-term moments and the long-term plans. When we look out for the interests of others, and we are the steady rock they can lean on in times of adversity. Building is not always flashy work. It is very hard work. However, the reward of a beautifully built relationship is experiencing happiness, fulfillment, contentment, and meaning.

Time is one way to measure how well something is built. Often, we think of Ally's grandparents who have been married for more than sixty-seven years. Their relationship was built strong enough to withstand the test of time. It's hard to overlook that their occupations are both related to building. Ally's grandfather was a genius electrical and digital engineer and manager, and her grandmother bought and sold real estate in the beach cities. They probably deployed the same techniques used to build their occupations in their relationship, and they did so systematically and intentionally so their marriage was built to last. They talk about coming home every day when, before eating or doing anything else, they would reconnect and talk about their days.

Today we have the opportunity to build with love and action. Not all relationships are equal, and each one should be given its own assessment and value. Sometimes areas of our relationships are neglected and damaged, and we should figuratively go in to conduct a thorough repair, making sure all the damage is removed and things are cleaned, repaired, or remodeled. Relationally, love is the best way to conduct any repairs. It is important to take the time and care to rebuild so the relationship is better than before.

What if every relationship had a master architect and an ultimate blueprint, but it was up to the two people in the relationship to figure that out? With our eternal calling in mind, let's build relationships that can withstand the test of time and of which our Master Architect would be proud.

BUILDING YOUR PROSPEROUS RELATIONAL LIFE

Write out your ideal relational vision that you would like to build toward, just as a builder draws up plans. How would you dialogue in the relationship? What would you think about the other person and how would you interact with them? How would you start to remodel or restore the weak points or challenges? Invite God to share His vision with you and help you think about what your relationships could be.

1. What are the values in and for one of your closest relationships?
2. How do you build bridges to become closer? Take time to dream and hope without restrictions. Even if you feel some of it is a bit unrealistic, it is important to stretch your mind and heart toward being aware of the best-case scenario.
3. What tools can you use to build the relationship from question one? (Ideas: giving money, giving time, listening, forgiving, reading books, attending workshops or counseling, asking others how they have built strong relationships and following their model.)
4. Pick one way to intentionally invest in that relationship today.
5. If you feel comfortable, share your relationship vision with the person you want to build it with.
6. Ask the other person if they have a relational vision.

PROSPERITY PRAYER

God, You are our Master Builder who holds the blueprints of our lives. Just as Noah built the ark, year after year as a representation of Your covenant with us, so we look to You for strategy, wisdom, and understanding on how we should build our relationships. The ark was covered in pitch within and without to make sure it did not spring a leak in times of testing. We want to cruise through our relationships just as Noah and his family did because the ark was so well built. We look to You as our Builder and Maker. Show us the vision of love that You have for us and for those around us.

CREATING HOLISTIC PROSPERITY

 Spiritual: Build your spiritual walk by using available tools, which might include prayer, meditation, asking, seeking, and knocking.

 Health: Build your health through eating well and caring for your body. You are the temple of the Holy Spirit; work to build a strong and God-honoring temple.

 Financial: Build your finances by using the tool of strategy. Consider how compound interest can build your finances or portfolio.

 Professional: Build your professional life with the tools of integrity, a good work ethic, and a strong network.

 Mindset: Build your thought life by only agreeing with thoughts that help you build your desired future, not ones that tear you down. Partner with your goals, not your shortcomings.

 Social: Build your social life by allowing yourself to be known by others, being curious about others to build bridges of understanding, and letting your guard down around trusted people.

2

Remembering Past Provision

"HAVING EYES, DO YOU NOT SEE? AND HAVING EARS, DO YOU NOT HEAR? And do you not remember, when I broke the five loaves for the five thousand, how many baskets full of broken pieces you picked up?" They said to Him, "Twelve."

—MARK 8:18–19

Looking back into past provision brings us the revelation that we already have an established testimony. John the Beloved was in the middle of the Revelation of Jesus, and he turned around when he heard a voice. Geographically, nothing was different behind him because he was in the middle of an encounter with God. The reason he needed to turn around is because he needed to look into the past to find out what God was saying and be reminded of what God had done.

God loves remembering past provision so much that one of the Holy Spirit's main jobs is to help us bring to remembrance all the things Christ has spoken. Also, He brings to our remembrance the promises He has generationally spoken over our family. God did this for the descendants of Abraham and reminded them of His promises. This provided them with hope, strength, and vision. They were able to connect, build, and grow with their family through recalling their past provision.

Often we are already equipped and empowered to overcome in our present season because God has already confirmed His testimony of breakthrough in our lives or the lives around us. One time Jesus was on a boat with His disciples, and they were complaining about not having food. Essentially, He said to them, "Do you not see? Can you not hear, and do you not remember when I broke the five loaves and fed five thousand? How many baskets full of food were left?" He was reminding them that their moment of provision was based on their ability to remember what God had done (Mark 8:18–19).

When we recall what He has already done in our lives, we have access to that same breakthrough in our present moment. God is the same yesterday, today, and forever. As we remember what He has done, we find the keys to victory for today. We can do this for our friends and family as well. What victories have they already walked through that they can be reminded about to help them in this season? Or, what has God done in your life that you can bring to their attention to encourage them?

Experience is a great teacher. One way that we can prosper is by remembering ways that our family or relationships impacted us for good. Imagine a mother demonstrating consistently that she is available to help when a child faces problems. She gives the provision of help, wisdom, insight, and relationship to the child despite the child's failures. Now imagine this same child grows up, gets married, and is facing relational problems with their spouse. Likely, if they remember the past relational wisdom and advice and provision provided by their mother, they will return to her at that time to receive help.

One key is to collect and remember the good memories and the provisions and deposits of love that have been given to you over your lifetime. From your brain's perspective, remembering something in detail or reimagining it brings the same feelings as when it actually occurred and makes it more likely for you to repeat that behavior. If you dwell on those good moments of relational provision, it changes how you feel about that person. Then this changes how you treat them in the moment, which creates a positive snowball effect on your relational health. It increases your gratitude for them, perhaps their gratitude for you, and your overall bond. You may not be able to see or hear, but you can always remember!

BUILDING YOUR PROSPEROUS RELATIONAL LIFE

How can you build a life of relational victories? Practice accepting the relational faults you've experienced in life. Remind yourself that dwelling on those thoughts may increase your suffering or frustration and usually will move you further away from prosperity. Instead try this:

1. Identify someone who has given relational provision to you. What did they do? What difference did it make? Dwell on this for a moment and thank God for it.
2. Identify the good. Don't have all-or-nothing thinking with relationships that went wrong. Often people become upset or

more disappointed thinking about good that didn't last. But good was there for a time, and you experienced it. There was some good in many relationships that no longer exist. Identify the good and be thankful for that successful season.

3. Identify one thing you can do today to create relational provision and legacy for a family member, friend, or someone in your community. This can be something you already do, but with your being mindful to be consistent and steadfast in it—things like offering advice, offering a safe place to talk, or offering hope.

PROSPERITY PRAYER

Holy Spirit, You bring to remembrance all things that Christ has spoken to us in the written Word or spoken word. You are the best at remembering. Thank You for instilling in us the key to our breakthrough in what You have already done. We turn around and look into our past to see what You have already completed and fulfilled. You alone are victorious in every area of life, and we bless You for giving us this way of provision. We will always remember what You have done.

CREATING HOLISTIC PROSPERITY

 Spiritual: Increase your trust and faith in God's ability to care for you.

 Health: Create a positive emotional state where you relive the positive emotions you felt when the provision first happened and gave you hope.

Financial: Give strength to keep doing your best to partner with the opportunities that come along financially.

 Professional: Provide strength and courage to pursue open doors and job opportunities from a place of assurance that God will provide like He did in the past.

 Mindset: Open your mind to think creatively about how that provision could be achieved again and steady your mind in times of uncertainty and doubt.

 Social: Increase the energy in a community to continue working toward growing the provision that has been provided.

3

Overcoming Challenges

He who overcomes, and he who keeps My deeds until the end, TO HIM I WILL GIVE AUTHORITY OVER THE NATIONS.

—REVELATION 2:26

It's impossible to have relationships without challenges. God knew from the beginning that we would inevitably encounter setbacks, roadblocks, and challenges in our relational journeys. We as humans have too much power and self-will to not be involved in challenges with one another and in life. Challenges come in big and small sizes, but there are great ways to overcome challenges in our relationships. First, let's look at this from God's perspective.

God is far too familiar with relational challenges. It took Adam and Eve all of twelve minutes to start a relational challenge with Him. After Eve was tempted, God implemented boundaries, a new code of conduct to preserve the broken relationship, and a redemptive plan for repair. He brought forth His blueprint for redemption of the relationship in Jesus. Since Jesus' sacrifice, two thousand years have passed with many challenges; nevertheless God has been an overcomer and victorious in the restoration.

Many of us face some of our biggest challenges in our closest relationships. The good news is, through His Word God has given us the same blueprint He used to help us overcome the challenges we face with family and friends. This is our model: to love through acceptance, boundaries, and planning. We accept our relationships for what they are and do not expect them to change. Then we are able to make decisions from a place of love, joy, peace, and patience. Acceptance of people as they are, not as the people you would like them to be, will reduce your stress and frustration.

God is with us, creating a way for us to be empowered and victorious in the struggles, battles, and setbacks. His grace is sufficient for us today. We can place our heads on the Rock of Jesus, just as Moses did, and hear the voice of heaven for guidance in our relational challenges (Exodus 33:21–22). Then we deploy an umbrella of curiosity to understand the conflict from the other person's perspective.

Next we form appropriate boundaries to protect ourselves and the other person in the conflict. These boundaries allow us to take care of ourselves. We can have emotional boundaries with others, as well as in actions and in communication. Then we work to become "trigger proof." Being trigger proof means that we can manage our feelings and reactions and mindsets, regardless of what anyone does, says, or implies. We do not give others the power to pull a trigger that causes us to explode.

Last, before we enter into any relational conflict, we must be consistent in sowing seeds of love to establish goodwill. Every relationship has challenges, but our response determines our character and emotional health. When we are vulnerable in our communication, we can defuse potential conflicts before they arise. Most challenges occur because of fear; someone fears being misunderstood or mistreated. Embrace them with love. Comfort them. Don't pull out your sword and go to battle. Instead, find a way to get to relational repair and allow God to lead you.

BUILDING YOUR PROSPEROUS RELATIONAL LIFE

It can be challenging to be around family members who share different values, interests, and perspectives. One way to overcome this is through empathy and perspective. Here are some ideas about how to relationally prosper:

1. Instead of challenging them, simply start asking questions and being curious about their thoughts, feelings, and emotions. To find a way forward, you have to truly understand them instead of assuming that you already do.
2. Whatever they say, don't take it personally! Seek to support them.
3. Resist the urge to solve their problems, judge them, or prove something. You may find they start to come to you for advice and ideas if you do not over-offer.
4. Ask God what He sees when He looks at them. Consider ways you can partner with the gifts, talents, and plans God has for them.

PROSPERITY PRAYER

God, You are an overcomer in life. You have had to overcome so many challenges. Thank You for being such a good model in life for how to overcome. Thank You for showing me Your blueprint of love and action that mends broken relationships and prevents future breakups. You are my Lord, Friend, and Guide. I boldly ask for Your wisdom in my relationships.

CREATING HOLISTIC PROSPERITY

 Spiritual: Jesus is the ultimate overcomer to relate to. Life is a spiritual journey during which you overcome challenges and strengthen your spirit to be more powerful. God wants to relate to you and take you through each trial and challenge. If you let Him, you will win the prize of knowing, understanding, and loving Him more for helping you overcome.

 Health: When you become victorious you have that to fall back on. You can increase emotional stability as well as faith and hope in your emotions (which lead to emotions in your body) as you remember what you have previously overcome.

 Financial: Increase your courage and confidence that you can overcome financial challenges by starting with small victories and building on those.

Professional: Work is often about problem solving. It is important to have plans A, B, and C. This leads to a greater likelihood of overcoming a given challenge instead of spending time coming up with one "perfect" plan that could be derailed.

 Mindset: Have the mindset that you are an overcomer and born in a time of adversity, but remember that with God nothing is impossible and nothing can stop you.

 Social: Love-based solutions are the bedrock of any progressive society. We were created to help others overcome through the power of God. We are uniquely situated to help the world prosper by building positive solutions to overcome the social challenges of our day.

4

Investing

So he who had received five talents came and brought five other talents, saying, "Lord, you delivered to me five talents; look, I have gained five more talents besides them." His lord said to him, "Well done, good and faithful servant; you were faithful over a few things, I will make you ruler over many things. Enter into the joy of your lord."

—Matthew 25:20–21 NKJV

We all have some understanding of investing, but have you ever considered the idea of investing in your relationships just as one would in the stock market? It's far too common for people to wander in their relationships without a clear direction, goal, and vision, leaving them with poor results. However, when we invest in our relationships, we change our approach toward them and therefore change the outcome. The extension of investing brings principles and practical processes with proven results.

Investing is not random; it is systematic, calculated, and thorough. Entertaining relationships without a plan that has measurable goals may lead to reactionary, confused, and frustrated people. Relationships are for building long-term mutual rewards like comradery, connection, productivity, and love. When we build and invest in something, it takes meticulous planning and strategy. Investing requires an initial and ongoing assessment for feasibility, practicality, and risk versus reward. If we determine that it is a good decision to invest, doing so requires strategy, patience, and nurturing.

The most valuable resource we have to invest is our time—even more than our money. We (Ally and Jeremy) invest every day in our relationship with intentional deposits of time. We learned early on that we can make small and large deposits, depositing encouragement, kindness, curiosity, understanding, and support of each other. We also make small deposits like sending text messages throughout the day, checking in before we make big purchases, working on a project together, planning a trip together, and stopping everything for an unplanned hug.

Love needs to be developed. Ideally, it grows over time. I (Ally) was never interested in falling in love. I felt the most successful, thriving, happy, empowering relationship would not sweep me off my feet in a moment only to drop me the next. In the beginning of my relationship with Jeremy, before allowing my emotions to get involved, I made lists of my values and Jeremy's values and looked to see how our lives, personalities, and future would likely progress. This was something I did to make sure my investment would likely bear long-term fruit. Love accumulates as we receive interest on our investment.

The world would say love is an emotional experience. In part that is true, but it should not be only emotional, and in fact, feeling emotionally in love is not what builds a strong relationship. Constant investments help make a relationship unshakable. We should plan time to invest in our families and friends by building an investment schedule. Some people feel that for relationships to be genuine we must be spontaneous about the time we spend with others. This mindset can prevent a person from investing regularly and consistently in relationships. You wouldn't expect the company you work for to spontaneously invest in your pay, or when it feels like it, nor would you spontaneously decide to go to work or only when you feel like it.

Where our treasure is, there our heart will be also. Place your treasure in the people around you. The people you love. Invest in those relationships to bear long-term fruit. Think about the concept of investing and use it in each relationship that you are pouring into weekly or monthly. Expect a return that is compounding. If you are depositing the invisible attributes of God like faith, hope, love, and joy, God will watch over your investments, and your reward will be like that in the parable of the talents.

BUILDING YOUR PROSPEROUS RELATIONAL LIFE

Take the time today to look at your next month and consider three people you want to make relational investments in.

1. Let them know you want to invest in them and ask if there is a way they would like you to do that.

2. If they don't know how you can invest in them, consider their love language (receiving gifts, quality time, physical touch, words of affirmation, or acts of service)[2] and create an investment that capitalizes on the way they feel loved.
3. Schedule when and how often you will make this investment.
4. Post your investments on the fridge or create an "investment bank" using a vase, box, or jar, where you can write down your planned intentional investments. This is for you to look at and remember. It is satisfying and motivating to have a visual representation of your investments and to watch them increase!

PROSPERITY PRAYER

Thank You, Jesus, for all Your relational investments. You provide us so many keys to relationally succeed. We are overwhelmed by Your constant, steady, well-planned, and reward-centered investment in us. You are truly a model for how we should live and how we should invest in others. We are blessed by You, Jesus, in more ways than can be counted. We love You.

CREATING HOLISTIC PROSPERITY

 Spiritual: Invest spiritually by sowing thoughts and time with the Father. Converse with Him with the written Word He has given. Look around to see things that represent His heart each day. Get to know His thoughts and mind.

Health: Consider that every food you eat is a good or bad investment in your future health.

 Financial: Consider the short- and long-term benefits of diversification in your investing. Investing 5 percent in twenty things as opposed to 100 percent in one thing provides tremendous financial protection. How many investments do you have?

 Professional: Always seek to grow your career. Never stop investing in growth, new directions, innovation, and learning.

 Mindset: Getting support to understand how to make your emotions more life giving and godly is a powerful investment. One way to do this is by speaking with a counselor, pastor, or therapist who can provide strategies about emotional issues.

 Social: Plant seeds in your community and local government to invest in resources, opportunities, and the well-being of your community. If you are expecting to reap a bountiful harvest in your social sphere, you must invest five times more first and demonstrate loyalty to tend to that "crop" on good and bad days.

5

Generosity

Now this I say, he who sows sparingly will also reap sparingly, and he who sows bountifully will also reap bountifully.

–2 Corinthians 9:6

The posture of bringing everything you have to each relationship is an extraordinary way to remain proactive while depositing healthy, fruitful interactions that bring a host of benefits to the collective unit. Generosity, one of God's greatest qualities, involves being abundant, and in this case being abundant with those around you. Generosity is powerful! Jesus showed us how generosity opened up entire cities for transformation. We can utilize this amazing tool set in our own lives and relationships.

Generosity is a currency, but it does not need to be restricted to financial generosity. Generosity is a way to prosper in every way in life. You can be generous with affection, thoughts, mood, time, and actions. When held in tension with doing what is right and pure, generosity is one of the best ways to open up the hearts of your family. It is one of the ways we express love. Within our families we can be generous with our tangible and invisible assets, our support, encouragement, legacy, and inheritance.

When we sow bountifully, we reap bountifully! The results of generosity are immeasurable. Generosity increases bonding, security, love, and gratitude in all parties involved—not just in the one who receives, but in the one who gives. When we give to others, we are subconsciously telling ourselves there is a reason we are giving. We start to think more fondly and affectionately toward those we give to. The one who gives gains as much—or more—as the one who receives. Giving impacts our brains on a deep level, what some refer to as a "giver's high"—our brains are so impacted that we have a tangible mood change. In fact, in some people, this has an addictive element.

We (Jeremy and Ally) both sow into our relationship with generous time, love, and care. We find that our relationship is in a constant state of abundance because we make consistent deposits throughout each interaction. It is much easier to overcome challenges, support each other, meet the needs and desires of others, and experience a deeper love because there is enough care and attention for both of us to thrive together. We have learned that if we lead with generosity, we will not even think about what divides us, because we are receiving good things consistently.

When people in your family are down emotionally, relationally, or financially, generosity can bring them back to life. We can be generous in our physical care, feedback, empowerment, emotional care, validation, support, encouragement, and insight. Most of these things don't cost us anything but time, and we should always make time for those we care about. We want to build up a reservoir of strength and hope in our family and friends so they can draw from it each and every day. Do you remember the example Jesus gave to the woman at the well? "But those who drink of the water that I will give them will never be thirsty" (John 4:14 NRSV). Jesus gave us a generous stream of life!

We can sow big and small seeds of generosity in our words, actions, and resources. It may seem counterintuitive to be giving so much with the expectation of prosperity, but that is God's way of increasing our connectivity to those around us. As we give, we open ourselves to receive more. Whenever we give, we should recognize that it will be given back to us. This is God's promise. May we be as generous to those around us as Jesus was and is to us.

BUILDING YOUR PROSPEROUS RELATIONAL LIFE

It is important to focus on giving what we have. Sometimes it helps to give things we feel we do not have enough of, with the expectation of God repaying.

1. Identify something you have that you can generously give to a relationship. Some ideas are affection, a positive mood, quality time, feedback, craftsmanship, attentive listening, gifts, acts of service, cooked meals, a ride, and so forth.
2. Identify something you do not feel you have much of that you want more of and can start to give out of your lack, such as patience, understanding, friendship, and hope.
3. Identify people you will give some of this to this week.

PROSPERITY PRAYER

Your abounding love, Jesus, fills up our hearts and minds more than we can handle. The earth can't even contain the blessing of Your testimony, it is so vast. You have been so generous with us, time and time again. We are like the little boy with a few loaves and fish, and You can multiply the little we offer. You are so generous. Thank You for training us and teaching us the kingdom ways of generosity.

CREATING HOLISTIC PROSPERITY

Spiritual: We are instructed to freely receive and freely give. As we give generously to the spiritual well-being of others, we align our hearts with God. By doing this we open up possibilities to receive more spiritually in our walk with God.

Health: Provide and receive emotional generosity by being a strong anchor and staying calm even when others are stressed or upset, giving them a safe place when you don't react to their emotions.

Financial: Just as with the ability to give love, you can give financially, which opens up hearts to share more with you.

Professional: Allow others to join in and benefit from a good process, not keeping skills and insights to yourself, but helping the new generation thrive through mentoring and teaching, solidifies you as an expert and resource in your field.

Mindset: Have a mindset that generosity is the gateway for transformation, for relationship, and for a healthy mind.

 Social: Sharing yourself and your gifts with others by contributing to your community can open doors for you and your community to prosper and be a sign of prosperity to others.

6

Expectations

According to my earnest expectation and hope,
that I will not be put to shame in anything, but
that with all boldness, Christ will even now, as
always, be exalted in my body, whether by life
or by death.

—PHILIPPIANS 1:20

*C*reating expectations leads to trust, and trust to fruitfulness. When we (Jeremy and Ally) started dating, I (Jeremy) created a scenario in which Ally knew what to expect from my heart, engagement level, thoughts, and intentions at all times. I overcommunicated my process and expectations so if any decisions needed to be made, Ally would not have to factor in any unknown variables. My expectations were clear. I worked to make it plain, and the guessing game was solved. Therefore, any disappointment and failed expectations were diminished.

Much of our relational frustration in life comes from creating expectations of what others should do and then struggling to overcome our disappointment when they don't perform. A healthy way of processing expectations is vital to relationships, bonding, and relational peace. It presents a big challenge when we do not communicate our expectations. For example, have you checked in with your family members about your expectations of them? Have you invited them into your process? If not, your expectations may not be healthy because they are based only on you, not on the partnership God created you to have with them. We must build expectations out of truth and relationship with gratitude, not out of wishful thinking.

We should reserve the option to have unmet expectations and still be okay. We don't have to be victims of our failed expectations of others. Some may have failed expectations of pastors who did not give them what they needed. But if the pastors weren't told about the expectations, they were powerless to help. This childish thinking is based on a hope to be fully known, loved, and understood without articulating our expectations in a clear way.

Some dream of the perfect person who will "just know" what they want or need, but this rarely happens, and that mindset is not a sign of relational empowerment or health. I know what Ally wants and needs often without her verbalizing it because she has communicated it in the past—not because I "just knew." Communicating expectations and needs is a sign of relational maturity and health. Withholding or expecting mind reading is not. This closeness only comes with long-term trust, relationship, and commitment; it does not often happen automatically. The same principles are true for relationships with parents and siblings. Look at historical data to predict and expect how people will act, not unfounded hopes for how they will respond.

When disappointed, revisit your expectation and examine it. Expectations can come from different places, including your past, media, and friends. Are your expectations grounded or ungrounded? Was your expectation based on history, displayed patterns, the relationship? Or was it based on something else? Practice realigning to what history has shown you and what your relationship partner communicates. Establish expectations together for optimal thriving.

How do we work through a failed expectation in our relationships? Two tools we (Jeremy and Ally) often use in our relationship are curiosity and suspending judgment. When we feel angry at each other, offended, rejected, upset, or get any message of relational disconnection in our emotions, we suspend our judgment and turn to curiosity. We will often say, "I felt disconnected when you said or did that. I am curious about what you meant." This opens a conversation that can lead to reconnection. Then we overcome by simply asking the other, "Can you help me resolve this feeling?" Sometimes we still disagree, but together we find a way to stay connected and peaceful in the midst of disagreement.

BUILDING YOUR PROSPEROUS RELATIONAL LIFE

Expectations often hide in words or phrases such as *should*, *better*, or even *What is wrong with you?* It is okay to expect things from the people closest to you, but expectations need to be created in a collaborative process based on the relationships, not on control or assumptions. Take time to examine your "shoulds."

1. Write out things that you think people should do: "Husbands should . . ."; "Wives should . . ."; "Children should . . ."; "Parents should . . ." These are expectations. They are not good or bad in themselves.

2. Ask yourself if the person is capable of doing those things you expect, if their history shows they are aware and able to do them, and if they even want to do them. We cannot control people into becoming our image of what we want and expect without hurting the relationship.

3. Communicate your expectations and see how the person responds. Maybe they do not feel they can meet the expectations. At that point, we may need to accept instead of expect. Focusing our energy on acceptance can be tremendously freeing.

4. Don't be powerless! Find other creative and healthy ways to meet your needs and expectations, or choose to let go.

PROSPERITY PRAYER

God, You have the healthiest expectations, and You are the best communicator on the planet. Teach us to create and process the best and most realistic expectations of ourselves and of the world around us. We love You, Jesus, and we love how You are a perfect model for tangible expectations. Bring us into the best relational expectations this year. Help us to have thriving relationships.

CREATING HOLISTIC PROSPERITY

 Spiritual: We should hope and expect to receive good things from God. Expect God to show up in your daily life, and you are more likely to see how He does. This will create a framework to see the redemptive and perfect will of God.

 Health: Have realistic expectations so that you can create change and build health in your body. It might not feel nice or fun, but if we expect negative consequences for our poor eating or other behaviors toward our bodies, we can be more powerful to impose changes to receive positive consequences for our healthy decisions.

 Financial: Pro forma statements create a way for a company to plan products, investments, and growth strategies because of the expectations set in place.

 Professional: It is vital for employees and employers to maintain and communicate realistic expectations (being paid, having predictable growth opportunities). This creates boundaries that bring life and longevity. A lack of expectations can create bitterness and resentment.

 Mindset: We should expect people to be good and expect great things for our life. If we don't, we will miss the opportunities for prosperity when they come. We should expect that we are worthy, there is hope, and we can do all things through Christ.

Social: Setting expectations for a community or group provides an anchoring point to build and grow from. If others don't know what to expect, it will be hard for them to feel they know and trust us. Creating expectations for an organization provides strength and unity. Write the vision and make it plain.

7

Prophetic Word

And the elders of the Jews were successful in building through the prophesying of Haggai the prophet and Zechariah the son of Iddo. And they finished building according to the command of the God of Israel and the decree of Cyrus, Darius, and Artaxerxes king of Persia.

—EZRA 6:14

Prophecy, also known as hearing God's voice and sharing it, is one of the most powerful gifts God has given humanity. One-third of the Bible is dedicated to prophecy! God invited us into this gift and has called us all to prophesy. "But even more I wish you could all prophesy" (1 Corinthians 14:5 NLT). Why? So we can hear His heart and speak His heart. Prophecy releases the very words and thoughts of God into a given person, place, or thing, thus releasing the same abundance and prosperity that Jesus released when He was here on the earth.

However, it seems the church is often confused about this subject. It is commonly misunderstood because of people's misuse and inability to find Jesus in their prophecy and because of a lack of education. There is a tangled web of judgment- and sin-oriented prophecy that is not from God. Apocalyptic fiction is often confused with prophecy because the book of Revelation talks about the apocalyptic unveiling of Jesus. Also, many people speak under the guise of prophecy but their words are not from God's heart. They are self-focused, and their motives are self-gain. All prophecy from God should point back to Jesus and usher in His wonderful nature.

Jesus is the creator of prophecy, and in Him all prophecies should abide. Most simply, prophecy is about love and sharing the encouragement, edification, and exhortation of God with others to direct and support their short-term and long-term futures. It is about God's plans for our lives. Jeremiah 33:3 says that if we call on Him, He will show us great and mighty things that we did not know previously. He wants to share His hopes, vision, and dreams with us so we can share with those around us.

As we grow in our ability to hear God and prophesy, we have the ability to tap into the possibilities of God for the people around us and for ourselves. We are not just building others up for the moment; we're also speaking into their futures. God discerns the thoughts and intentions of the heart and wants to share them with us. We can share that message with our families. We can share with them about their callings, dreams, and desires and invite them into what God has for them.

Jeremy often asks God what He thinks of one of his friends or family members. Jeremy asks questions that will unlock God's heart about that person. He waits and writes down what he hears and then finds the best way to share it with them. This should be a normal part of life. God always speaks, and we should find out what He is saying. Prophecy is to help guide us into our future with the vision and plan to succeed.

With any prophecy, we should consider the interpretation and delivery. Our interpretation might not be the best one, so we should submit the word without our own filter. The delivery of the word should be with humility, not in boasting. We should use soft words that invite the listener in rather than declaring that we heard something from God and saying, "God said." If we are wrong, we are wrong, not God. So refrain from saying "God said," and have faith in God's ability to speak through you. Speak forth what you hear for your friends and family. Share the heart of God with them and partner with them to walk into the abundance that God has for them!

BUILDING YOUR PROSPEROUS RELATIONAL LIFE

Prophesy hope to someone (or everyone) in your family today. Think of the impact of your words on eternity. Think of the investment you will make in helping your family stay strong and reach their potential.

1. Spend a few minutes in prayer asking God to help you give your family encouraging words.
2. Write an email, write a letter, or call and ask to share the encouragement. Maybe you don't mention God because that would be something they would be frustrated by or angry about. Maybe you do mention God somehow, but either way, you are God's agent to release hope, and that hope carries a connection to God that will impact the person's soul.

3. Continue to pray these things over them and ask God to show you ways to help them come to life in these areas.

PROSPERITY PRAYER

God, You are so pure and just. You speak the words of life! Thank You for declaring over us the abundance of Your voice. We love Your words and cherish them. We are so thankful for Your prophetic nature and ask You to release us in this. We want to speak forth the words of life that You give. Share with us Your heart and mind so we can invite others in. Thank You, Lord, for Your love.

CREATING HOLISTIC PROSPERITY

 Spiritual: A prophetic word helps you grow closer to God and increases trust, knowing that God knows your life, knows what is ahead before it happens, and wants to tell you about it.

 Health: Prophetic words can help motivate you to change behavior and help you know that God is partnering with you on your health journey!

 Financial: The testimony of Jesus is the spirit of prophecy. His testimony prophesies that all our needs will be cared for as we work with God and invite God into our life, process, and finances, looking for ways to actively partner with provision.

Professional: God can provide a prophetic word to help direct you toward a certain career or job opportunity. He can give you prophetic insight into strategies to help your business, customers, and bosses.

 Mindset: Part of the power of a prophetic word is that it helps us change our minds about ourselves, God, and our futures. This causes us to change our behavior in the present to align with our future selves.

 Social: Prophecy has the power to provide healing, hope, restoration, and vision to a community.

PART 2

Increasing Spiritual Prosperity

Spiritual prosperity is all about coming face-to-face with the life-transforming God. We are spirit before we are flesh. A strong spirit impacts every part of who we are. When our spirit is alive and empowered, it can accomplish things that cannot otherwise be accomplished. It can see things that cannot otherwise be seen. It can help us do things that cannot otherwise be done. It is a life force. Our connection with God and His wonderful kingdom comes to us by the Holy Spirit. Through genuine spiritual relationships, we start to experience the fruit of the Spirit. Life begins to bloom with love, joy, and peace without any striving as we follow God's principles that lead us to His active voice, bringing transformation to every area of life.

Perspective

So he answered, "Do not fear, for those who are with us are more than those who are with them." Then Elisha prayed and said, "O Lord, I pray, open his eyes that he may see." And the Lord opened the servant's eyes and he saw; and behold, the mountain was full of horses and chariots of fire all around Elisha.

–2 Kings 6:16–17

God is spirit, and He made us in His image; therefore, we should consider our spiritual journey to be top priority. The servant in 2 Kings, like you and me sometimes, was having a very natural moment. He was using his natural perspective of known interpretations and truths to conclude that he was in big trouble. Then Elisha introduced a different reality by changing the servant's perspective with a perspective that was spiritual and established in God. This changed everything; the servant's countenance, heart, and options all changed in one moment.

Our perspective can be both natural and spiritual. We have a natural perspective about everything: how we think TVs are made, how to drive a car, and how clean the airport should be. The construct of our experience builds our natural and spiritual perspectives. Our experiences, mighty and small, victorious and terrible, have formed our perspective on life. In turn, that perspective is the steering wheel to all our decisions and possibilities.

God, knowing every facet of how we are made, hardwired us for His perspective. He has given us access to His thought bank, the mind of Christ, so we can share in His perspective. We can begin to connect with God and gain insight and access to His experience. When we lift up our eyes, spiritually speaking, we are lifted up to a different altitude in thought. The perception of our natural problems gets smaller, and the expanse of God's goodness and possibility gets bigger.

A decade ago, I (Jeremy) went to ministry school for three years. When I was in the first year, I realized my limited experience and knowledge gave me a shortsighted spiritual perspective. Over the years in school, I would allow the stories, teaching, and Word of God to wash over my mind and change my thoughts and beliefs about God and myself. I was starting to form my eternal perspective about who God is and what God thought of me. My thoughts about the future and myself would change every time I changed my thoughts about God. This would then directly change how I related to people, how I acted, and the options I saw as possible. When I would meet someone for the first time, I began to ask God about His thoughts toward the person rather than just forming a natural opinion. I would ask God (who is outside of time) to tell me about the person's kingdom callings, giftings, and life.

This multifaceted perspective changed everything for me, just as it did for the servant in 2 Kings. I realized that when my thoughts are seen only through a natural lens, my perspective is very limited, but when I start to see my life through His eyes, His possibility becomes my opportunity. I stopped living for myself and started living with God in mind. His kingdom's purpose and plans became my purpose and plans.

When we have a spiritual perspective encompassed by His plans, the Bible becomes not just a historical document but a multi-dimensional invitation into our present experience with God. God has always referenced Himself, us, and the kingdom in spiritual dimensions in countless ways. We are spirit, soul, and body. He has given us faith, hope, and love. The Bible speaks of a first, second, and third heaven (2 Corinthians 12:2–4). In every situation in life, we are given the great invitation to see our lives from His perspective.

Jesus said to pray this way: "Our Father who is in heaven" (Matthew 6:9). That is the spiritual perspective that will bring us through any trial. Our Father is in heaven. What does He see? What is He doing? God wants us to see the dimensions of possibility by setting our mind on the things above.

BUILDING YOUR PROSPEROUS SPIRITUAL LIFE

What story do you tell yourself about yourself? The story you tell is the story you act out. Create a story about your life so far, about God, and about your future from a positive and realistic perspective. View it as a chance to practice seeing what God's perspective might be.

1. Identify a current challenge or fear you are facing and write it out like a story.
2. Ask God to help you imagine what happens next in the story and to help you see it the way He sees it.
3. Write out a perspective you have about yourself that is unhelpful.
4. Ask God to give you ideas to write a story about how you overcame the unhelpful thoughts. Write it as if it has already happened. If you're stuck, think about how someone else might overcome or did overcome and write your story to mirror that.

You don't have to fully believe things will happen the way you wrote them. This exercise is simply meant to open your mind to make room for new possibilities and God's perspective.

PROSPERITY PRAYER

Thank You, Jesus, for Your heavenly perspective. Take us up on the wings of eagles to see things Your way. You alone are victorious over every area in life. Bring us into the cleft of the rock, just as You placed Moses, to see things from Your eyes. Shape and mold our perspective to always look to the Father, just like You do, Jesus. Lead our eyes to find the good in all that You do in our lives. Bless You, Jesus.

CREATING HOLISTIC PROSPERITY

 Relationships and Family: Celebrate small changes as victories; families are long term.

Health: Realistic optimism about people and situations will bring about mental and emotional health.

 Financial: Assess purchases based on long-term perspective and planning. Will your purchase still be adding value to you next year? Assess why you are purchasing anything that costs more than one thousand dollars.

 Professional: Pursue the perspective of your supervisors or clients nondefensively. It could help you learn valuable information to gain the professional life you want. Doing better in their eyes is important.

 Mindset: Have the perspective that you can problem solve and overcome challenges. God has uniquely prepared you for any problem you face, and you can find a way.

Social: Know that the perspectives of others are sometimes built on experiences, fears, and other things. Be aware of those perspectives. Accept that others have different perspectives that may be valid based on their experiences and relationship with God, and those perspectives may also be different from yours.

9

Names of God

May his name endure forever;
May his name increase as long as the sun
   shines;
And let men bless themselves by him;
Let all nations call him blessed.
   —Psalm 72:17

Biblically, the names of God are an invitation into the nature of God. By definition, each name of God is a record of His character, will, intent, and history. They could also be considered the roles of God, the things He is found actively doing. Historically, we can read about how Jesus provided for people, but if His name is Provider and He never changed, then He is still our Provider today, right?

Absolutely! We simply need to know this by studying the Word of God and partnering with Jesus as our Provider.

Many are quick to adopt Jesus as their Savior because that name is the main theme of every Christian denomination for the past one hundred years. However, only a few call upon Him as their Healer, Creator, and Supplier, even though those are also His names. Therefore, the Bible invites us to call upon the name of Jesus for all we need. In the name of Jesus we are given all provision, direction, and sustenance.

When I (Jeremy) was a teen, I had a Names of God poster printed by John Paul Jackson's ministry. It boldly showed most of the popular names of God (there are more names of God than the poster could handle): Elohim, my Creator; Jehovah, my Lord God; El Shaddai, my Supplier; Adonai, my Master; Jehovah-jireh, my Provider. The list of names flowed across the poster. I would sit in contemplative prayer and ask God to reveal His nature through the names, saying, "Would You reveal Yourself to me as my Provider, my Supplier, my Savior?" This season opened the nature of God in new ways for me, which has forever changed my perspective on provision.

Understanding always brings access. The Bible says people perish for a lack of understanding (Hosea 4:6). When we recognize God as the source for our area of need, we gain access to a world of possibilities and solutions. God watches over His Word attentively to ensure it goes forth and performs what He spoke. His words do not come back to Him void!

One of the best forms of prayer is to declare who God is back to Him. It may sound silly, but prayer is not some magical set of words. It is about aligning our thoughts, will, emotions, and life to be like Jesus. As we declare who God is, we start to believe it, and when we believe it, we experience it, and when we experience it, so do the people around us. Faith comes by hearing the Word of God, perhaps out of our own mouths.

We should all become students of the Word. Study the Word of God to learn the different names of God. Last, we want to share one of our favorite names of God. Moses was presented with the Name above all names when God spoke to him and said, "I Am That I Am" (Exodus 3:14 KJV). He was telling Moses that He would be whatever Moses needed Him to be whenever Moses needed Him to be it. What an all-encompassing name of God! He will be our God in all ways. Lean on Him, trust Him, and call upon His name.

BUILDING YOUR PROSPEROUS SPIRITUAL LIFE

Becoming a student allows us to receive from the teacher. If we don't study for experience and connection with God, we are going to miss things about Him, things that could transform us. Read about each name of God until it is alive in you.

1. Consider two names of God that stand out to you in the list above or in your Bible.
2. Write about what it would be like to fully realize each considered aspect of God in every area of your life: spiritually, emotionally, relationally, and so on.
3. How can you be the hands and feet of God and demonstrate one of His names to someone today?

PROSPERITY PRAYER

You are the God above all other gods. We invite You in to reveal Yourself. We are filled with awe and adoration of Your loving ways. Help us to see Your name. Who are You showing us to be right now? May we forever see the fullness of Your name in all the areas of our life. We bless You, Jesus, and call upon Your name day and night.

CREATING HOLISTIC PROSPERITY

 Relationships and Family: One of God's names is Father God or Abba. This name reminds us that we are never without a father's love. Part of how we reveal the love of God is through fathering and mothering others (even if we are younger than they are).

 Health: Jehovah-rapha is the name of God that means "the God who heals you." Jehovah-shammah means "God my strength." God wants to provide us emotional healing, vitality, and strength.

 Financial: Jehovah-jireh is a name of God that means "Provider." God wants to provide for you.

 Professional: Jehovah-nissi means "Banner of Love." God wants to hold over you His banner of love in your work.

 Mindset: El Shaddai means "God who is sufficient." God is sufficient to fill your mind with truth, love, and hope.

 Social: Jehovah means "the God who is near." This reminds us that to imitate God, we must draw near to Him and to others as well.

10

Multiple Streams

Send your grain across the seas,
and in time, profits will flow back to you.
But divide your investments among many
    places,
for you do not know what risks might lie
    ahead.
    —Ecclesiastes 11:1-2 nlt

In 2018, we stood in the Klementinum, a breathtakingly beautiful, ancient library that opened in 1722 in Prague. The library had multiple stories full of old theology books, the center of the building was open, and you could see all the way up to the top floor and the ceiling, where a mural was painted. Philosophers, theologians, and angels were all pointing to the far end of the room toward a painting of Jesus. The words read, "In Him is all Knowledge." Our hearts melted with resounding agreement. I (Jeremy) thought about the words of Simon Peter, "Lord, to whom shall we go? You have words of eternal life" (John 6:68).

There are many avenues in which we can receive spiritual teaching, perspective, and prayer, and we need to be open to one person not having it all. This is what the apostle Paul talked about when people were arguing about who they followed. If we follow Jesus, we should look to the entire body of Jesus Christ for what it brings. Everyone has a different experience that we can glean from. We all see the world differently and carry God's revelation through our own understanding.

We are creatures of habit. If something is familiar, we stick with it. This is why advertisements work. We see something and then later choose it simply because we saw it before, not because it is better. We go to the same coffee shops every day and the same churches on Sunday. This is a wonderful thing, to an extent. But in addition to the comfort of our traditions, there is a whole world out there. In the beginning four streams flowed out of the garden of Eden. Why not just one? Because there are many ways God desires for us to grow with Him.

God can use anyone to bring forth His word. In the Bible He used children, women, men, rocks, and a donkey to convey timely messages! We should not limit God by saying He can only speak to us through one or two vessels. God not only wants to break you free from any religious traditions that keep you from His active voice but also to deliver an upgrade in your connection with humanity and Him.

Love provides the foundation of acceptance even when someone has ideas that might be different from yours. Our ability to learn from people should not be tethered around needing

100 percent agreement. Jesus had a very different philosophy and theology than most of the people He spent time with. As many have said, Jesus did a great job of "eating the meat and spitting out the bones."

God has many streams for us to connect with Him. Find His active voice wherever you go. When we realize just how big God is, we can connect with Him in new ways. We can see and understand the majesty, divine creativity, and power of God differently in every stream. Often the diversity confirms what Scripture says by bringing to light the complexity and all-encompassing nature of God. "Since what can be known about God is evident among them, because God has shown it to them" (Romans 1:19 HCSB).

BUILDING YOUR PROSPEROUS SPIRITUAL LIFE

Creating multiple streams works with friend groups, community groups, finances, and professional life. Here are a few ideas to start creating more spiritual streams:

- Spend a few minutes writing down the current streams of connection you have with God (for example, worship, prayer, Bible reading, going to church, and small groups).
- Read biographies of people of faith.
- Notice how God communicates to us through nature.
- Learn new meditation strategies to connect with God and meditate on His Word.
- Take an online class or course and ask what you can learn about God's nature through what you study.
- Go on a spiritual retreat.

PROSPERITY PRAYER

In You, Jesus, we find the streams of life. You alone show us a thousand ways to connect with You. Thank You, Jesus, for leading us so well that we can find You in everything You created. We can find You anywhere! Thank You for clearly revealing Yourself. Wherever we go, there You are. Thank You for always being there for us.

CREATING HOLISTIC PROSPERITY

 Relationships and Family: Be open to seeing others as complex, talented, and gifted in multiple ways. Instead of projecting wants or needs on them, be open to receiving who and what they are, without expectation of the narrow stream of who you want them to be.

 Health: Be open to bettering your health through multiple streams. Physical and emotional health can be enhanced by learning from various sources, receiving feedback, and trying new things.

 Financial: Every person will prosper the most when they develop seven healthy and prosperous streams of income. Having only one way to generate income is less than God promised and puts you under life-altering financial pressure, fear, or uncertainty every time that one stream is threatened.

Professional: Every company should consider each product or service in multiple ways and create new options without new services or products. Continue to find ways to use what you have in different ways to serve different demographics.

 Mindset: Wisdom comes in many forms. Train your ears for it, and rather than judging the source, judge if God may be trying to speak to you in many ways.

 Social: Increasing your social circles increases your experience in life. There are more than two dozen kinds of friendships, and you should be open to building friendships with more than those people who are like you. We have much to learn and prosper in when we expand our connections.

11

Abiding

If you abide in Me, and My words abide in you, ask whatever you wish, and it will be done for you.

—JOHN 15:7

God's ways to spiritually prosper are incredible. He gives us a diverse road map to abound in our connection with Him. We can act in steps of faith to create opportunities, we can work really hard to bring forth fruit, or—my favorite way—we can simply hang out with Jesus. Hanging out, or abiding, with Jesus can become the most fulfilling, rewarding, and prosperous time of your life.

The fruit of a tree does not get to full harvest by striving but by abiding. An orange doesn't pray or fast any harder than the next orange to get what it needs to thrive. It simply hangs on and abides in the vine (or tree). It doesn't sweat or toil to collect more nutrition; it just receives. The orange comes to full term not by works but by the strength of the source. This process of abiding is the same for us.

As we abide in the vine, just as Jesus has instructed us, we receive His nutrition and sustenance for our spiritual journey. We are connected to the source, plugged in not by our works but by His grace in our connection. Like John the Beloved, we shall lean on Jesus' chest and listen to His heart. Our spiritual fruitfulness comes by our proximity to Jesus. You have to be close to someone to listen to their heart. When you hear their heart, you are connected to the lifeline of who they are.

Every night for more than two years, I (Jeremy) intentionally set aside time to be with God and nothing else. I would lie down on the ground and simply invite Him in. I wouldn't pray in deep intercession or strive to produce some experience. I would not tell God all the things I needed. I simply invited Him into my body, my mind, my heart, and my emotions. My goal was to become so receptive to His love that I would find myself abiding in it. God showed up in marvelous ways every night. His presence would come into my room and overtake me. God would work on all my doubts and fears and share His promises with me. He would repair the broken places of my heart. He was truly abiding with me. My life became orchestrated by His love.

Abiding gives us an unspoken upgrade. We don't necessarily see it in the moment, but looking back, we see its direct impact on our mind, will, emotions, and relationships. That is the goal of our faith: connection to the Father. We begin to abound in our pursuit of heaven because we are connected. Jesus showed us that it is possible for one man in right relationship with the Father to maintain a deep, personal connection. Jesus did not miss one beat of the Father's heart. He was so connected that His actions were perfectly in sync with the Father's.

The by-product of abiding in Jesus is that He starts to live in you. His words spring up wellsprings of life. Then God comes along and says, "I see you have My words living in you. Speak what you wish, and it will be done for you. Dream whatever you may dream, and I will bring it forth. Pray whatever you may pray, and I will answer it." God is that good, and as we abide in Him, we will taste and see His goodness every day.

BUILDING YOUR PROSPEROUS SPIRITUAL LIFE

Abiding is a biblical form of meditation. One way to abide is through what some refer to as "soaking." Here is how you can abide today:

1. Take time to worship God and invite your heart to be aware of His presence. Think about His nature. Think about His love.
2. Lie or sit while knowing you are in the presence of God, and listen to quiet or contemplative songs about God's goodness.
3. Use your imagination and ask God to bring to mind pictures or ideas that remind you of His peace, protection, and plan for your life. Don't worry if your mind wanders; that is okay.
4. Spend twenty or more minutes doing this. The more you do it, the easier it will be to get to this place where you are aware of God and abiding in Him in your everyday life.

PROSPERITY PRAYER

Simplicity of love is what You call us to. We welcome You in without condition. We welcome You in without striving. Allow us to become the fruit of the vine. Permit us to dwell in the abundance of

Your grace and mercy. Make our hearts to be conditioned with love, and guide our paths to never lose the sense of Your warm embrace. We bless You, God.

CREATING HOLISTIC PROSPERITY

 Relationships and Family: Abiding in the love of God allows you to access deeper love for those you encounter, including your family and friends.

 Health: Abiding in the love of God brings peace beyond understanding to your emotions and actions. As you accept His love for your body, you create healthier habits for your body.

 Financial: Abiding in God allows you to think clearly and powerfully about good financial investments and how best to spend your resources.

 Professional: Abiding in or immersing yourself in an idea gives you the time and energy to pursue it wholeheartedly and succeed.

 Mindset: Abiding in thoughts of faith, peace, hope, and love transforms your mind to receive more of those things in your life.

 Social: Abiding in God can help you see the gifts, talents, and skills of others and help encourage them toward where they can apply and use them, which makes your community stronger.

12

Hidden Manna

He rained down manna upon them to eat
And gave them food from heaven.
—PSALM 78:24

In the Old Testament, the Lord said to Moses, "I will rain down bread from heaven for you" (Exodus 16:4 NIV). Israel was hungry in the wilderness, and God gave them a daily supply of manna. This was not only a prayer fulfilled to fill their bellies but also a sign from God of what He would bring through Jesus. The manna to Israel was an important temporary meal that sustained them during their years in the wilderness. It was glorious.

The act of daily provision was introduced through manna by the Father to take care of His kids. He loved them so much that He gave them supernatural provision from heaven to sustain them. Then Jesus came onto the scene and announced to the world that He is the Bread of Life, the bread that came down from heaven, the bread served in the tabernacle and temple. He is the daily provision. He is the perfect fulfilment to what was foreshadowed in years past. He is the source of Israel's provision. Jesus then invited everyone into this idea, saying to "pray, then, in this way" in Matthew 6:9–13: "Our Father who is in heaven. . . . give us this day our daily bread."

That prayer is alive and well today! It's an invitation for us to ask and receive the daily provision from heaven. John the Beloved believed it. He had an encounter with God and wrote about it for us to see the testimony of Jesus lived out. In the book of Revelation, John wrote of the hidden manna coming down from heaven for the Lord's bondservants. Bond servants are those who fall in love with their master after their debt is paid in full. We can be bond servants of Jesus Christ. We owe a debt (sin) we cannot pay, and He pays a debt that He does not owe (the cross).

God wants us to receive that supernatural daily provision that He gave to so many before us. We first need to lean on the chest of Jesus and hear His heartbeat. After we fall so in love with Him, He will invite us under His covering and place us in the cleft of the Rock (Jesus) and provide for us like fresh manna coming from the sky each morning. This is the by-product of an intimate relationship with the Father. He loves giving to His kids this way.

I (Jeremy) was invited by God through a series of dreams into a wonderful, life-changing internship with Pastor Bill Johnson of Bethel in Redding, California, where I could travel the world and learn from some of the best teachers in the church at the time. In the first dream, I was in heaven and being escorted around by Maria Woodworth-Etter (a past revivalist). She showed me a room in heaven filled with invisible, tangible boxes, saying, "You can have this room for twenty thousand dollars." I woke from the dream thinking it was souls or salvations I needed to achieve.

I felt led to speak to Pastor Bill about this. I said nothing about the dream but simply asked, "What would it take to intern for you? What would I need to do?"

Pastor Bill responded, "It will cost you about twenty thousand dollars for travel expenses." I was stunned and in awe! It was confirmation! I then quit my job with five hundred dollars in the bank, and God supernaturally supplied checks in the mail and random gifts for an entire year. I did not tell anyone about my financial need. No email, verbal request, or support letter went out, ever. Checks came in from random people who felt led to give (sometimes the day before my bills were due). That is hidden manna. God wants to show you seasons of hidden manna too! Draw near and ask for provision to accompany the vision God is giving you. He is our Provider.

BUILDING YOUR PROSPEROUS SPIRITUAL LIFE

Hidden manna is a by-product of a deep and fruitful relationship with Jesus. Here are some steps to receive hidden manna:

1. Posture yourself as a bond servant of Jesus.
2. Inquire of God regarding your daily needs, and ask Him what the daily needs are that He is providing and wants to provide.
3. Continue steadfastly in activities that engage your awareness of God's daily provision. Trust God in the process, even when the manna is not presented how you might guess it would be.
4. Acknowledge and thank God for the daily provision, no matter how small, to become more aware of the way He provides for you.

PROSPERITY PRAYER

You are our Provider, and You delight in providing for us, just as any good father delights in the ability to share with and care for his children. Your care to provide for me makes my heart sing with happiness and helps me experience Your love. I want to open my eyes to the hidden manna all around me—the financial, emotional, and spiritual food You provide to sustain, empower, and strengthen me in any situation.

CREATING HOLISTIC PROSPERITY

 Relationships and Family: If you are open to it, Jesus can provide you with new relationships out of nowhere that appear fully formed and produce good fruit in your life.

 Health: You can receive daily supernatural provision and soothing balm for your emotional health each day. As your cells are regenerated, God gives physical and emotional nutrition to sustain a new and thriving life.

 Financial: With an applied vision, His provision comes to supernaturally confirm His vision and words for your life and your prosperity. This includes unexpected donations, checks in the mail, expenses decreased, and so forth.

 Mindset: We are to die daily to our thoughts of who we are and receive the daily provision of Jesus' thoughts about us.

Social: God can remind you of social connections who can open doors of provision (relationships, other connections, services you need, access you need, or job opportunities).

13

Labor

Wealth obtained by fraud dwindles,
But the one who gathers by labor
increases it.

—PROVERBS 13:11

In the beginning Adam and Eve were called into a unique partnership with God. God called them to labor over what He had given them. They were to work in the field, just like gardeners. This invitation also tied into the process of the two people becoming fruitful and bringing forth a child by Eve going into labor. The kingdom of heaven is not realized in passivity but in work. "Jesus said to them, 'My Father is always at his work to this very day, and I too am working'" (John 5:17 NIV).

Just as we would labor in our gardens or in our nine-to-five jobs, we are invited to labor in the spirit. We are spirit before we are flesh. Sometimes when we are invited into a new season or we see what is possible in the Spirit, we need to push forth to the high calling of God in our lives. The Bible asks us to pray without ceasing and take the kingdom of heaven by force though fervency and persistence (1 Thessalonians 5:17; Matthew 11:12). We shall press into heaven until we see a breakthrough.

Intercession is a form of persistent prayer derived from frequent examples in the Old Testament. People would gather together to rend heaven over an issue that they knew was in God's heart. Modern-day intercessors demonstrate this type of labor over issues like abortion, slavery, or saving souls.

In Daniel 10:12–13 we see Daniel entering into spiritual labor followed by his breakthrough. "'Do not be afraid, Daniel,' he said, 'for from the first day that you purposed to understand and to humble yourself before your God, your words were heard, and I have come in response to them. However, the prince of the kingdom of Persia opposed me for twenty-one days. Then Michael, one of the chief princes, came to help me'" (BSB). Even heaven is in labor over our prayers to bring them about.

What does labor get you spiritually? Spiritual gifts are freely available, but God asks us to passionately pursue spiritual gifts. To actually capitalize on what is offered will cost time and effort. We will receive a greater benefit with greater efforts as we increase our pursuit and labor into something. The kingdom of heaven is violent, and the violent take it by force (Matthew 11:12). It is not a passive process like buying a lottery ticket.

Here are practical ways we can spiritually engage heaven and labor into the promises of God: (1) faithfully pursue our calling through devotion and action, (2) actively meditate on God's Word, (3) work hard to enter into His presence daily, and (4) digest the Word of God daily and hear what God is saying for our life, friends, and those around us. This will be labor intensive but extraordinarily rewarding.

BUILDING YOUR PROSPEROUS SPIRITUAL LIFE

One way to maximize your prayer life is to identify areas in God's heart that you can pursue with Him. The Father takes great pleasure in your pursuit and labor pertaining to the reward of Jesus. Here are ways that you can practically push in and utilize labor in your spiritual journey:

1. Write down injustices you have become aware of that are near and dear to your heart.
2. Pursue breakthroughs over those injustices in three different ways: prayer, collaboration with others, and educating others about the problem (online or in written or spoken form).
3. Test your anointing by contending for breakthrough in spiritual ways.

PROSPERITY PRAYER

Jesus, we love how You worked so hard to get close to us. A long time ago, You introduced us to a partnership with labor and what it could produce. Thank You for showing us how to press on toward the high call of God in our lives. Thank You for showing us the reward of all our labor—it's You. We delight in laboring for Your heart in our lives. Help us to forge ahead into the breakthroughs that You have called us to.

CREATING HOLISTIC PROSPERITY

 Relationships and Family: Laboring together creates connectedness, meaning, memories to share, and an opportunity to get to know people in new ways. Inviting others into your work around the house, into arts and crafts, or into events outside the home provides connecting points for relationships.

 Health: Changing destructive mindsets takes hard work. It is not intuitive at first. To receive strength and health, we have to strive and labor toward changing our mindsets about working out, diet, and unhelpful emotional reactions .

 Financial: Entering into labor is a beautiful way to partner in finances. You attain your goals and milestones as you partner in the work.

 Professional: One does not have to be an expert in a field. The person who is the best at the end of the day is the person who works hardest. Being willing to do the hard work is the most valuable asset you can offer, and in doing so you will outpace those around you.

 Mindset: Strive toward having the mindset that you have to labor to learn more. Having a mindset of being an expert and not having to learn disempowers your potential to achieve more.

Social: Laboring toward common goals helps us to thrive, as each person brings their skills and gifts to accomplish greater things and enter into greater prosperity than ever before. This can be serving and working with your city as well, by offering to clean public areas or sponsoring the refurbishing of a park or common area.

14

Glory

But the LORD will rise upon you
And His glory will appear upon you.
Nations will come to your light,
And kings to the brightness of your rising.

. . . Then you will see and be radiant,
And your heart will thrill and rejoice;
Because the abundance of the sea will be
*   turned to you,*
The wealth of the nations will come to you.
—ISAIAH 60:2–3, 5

God's glory is His nature in tangible form. The Bible declares the Lord will rise upon you and His glory, or nature, will appear upon you. When His glory is in the room, we get the best that heaven has to offer. The Father's abundant nature comes forth, and the abundance of the sea turns to you, and the wealth of the nations comes to you. Everything changes when God's glory is seen, realized, and felt! We welcome You, Jesus!

The glory of God can be hard to understand. For many it may feel intangible. But if we remove all associations we have with the word *glory*, we start to realize the point is that God's nature is known through His glory. We all want to be closer to His nature and closer to God. When we invite Him in the way He has described, we get to see and experience the abundance of the love of the Father. His heart comes forth, and we access the blessings of a good Father.

Sometimes His glory is tangible in the sense that our bodies and minds react to it in different ways than we would if the glory of God were not there. The glory of God can transform us and connect us more deeply with Him. Ally experiences His glory and transformation when she feels wrapped in the warmth and peace of God, and it feels like her mind and heart are being transformed with love. She also sees the glory of God through sunsets; every time she sees one, she feels connected to God and His thoughts, plan, and purpose.

There are different kinds of glory. The Bible even describes glory that scared people. All the kinds of glory have different purposes, but they help us get to know the characteristics of God. His glory is how He makes Himself available to us and makes the kingdom of heaven more tangible on the earth. When we are caught up in a moment of His glory, we feel awe, inspiration, and love. It is not some mysterious experience as much as God making Himself known. When His glory is present, the veil between heaven and earth is thinner and possibilities are greater for miracles and for His manifest presence to be known and experienced.

I (Jeremy) have traveled extensively for ministry during the last decade and have been connected to people who devote their lives to experiencing and connecting with God's glory. There are thousands of stories of times when God comes into the room and everyone gets an upgrade—even bigger upgrades than what Oprah can provide. God shows off His nature in radical miracles, salvations, signs and wonders, and experiences that blow our minds. These manifestations all let us into God's heart even more. We don't pursue the signs, but we enjoy them because they lead us to the Father.

God's glory is everywhere His nature is. The more we are open to experiencing His nature in the middle of our days, the more we will see His nature in the middle of our days. Remember, He doesn't need to change for us. We need to change to adapt to Him. But when we do, we will be properly aligned and unlock our greatest asset: the Father of heaven and earth. He wants to reveal Himself to us in everything we do. Let's press into His glory.

BUILDING YOUR PROSPEROUS SPIRITUAL LIFE

God's glory comes out of relationships. We need to increase our connection with God by improving our quality time and opportunities to experience His presence. You can practically pursue God's glory by doing the following things:

- Schedule an uninterrupted time every week to lie down and ask for the love of God to come into the room so you can experience it.
- Look actively for signs of God's glory around you in nature, in people, and in yourself.
- Pursue God's glory with others. Learn from them how they experience the glory of God. There are many churches, teachings, and conferences that spend time pursuing the glory of God. Consider attending at least one.

PROSPERITY PRAYER

Thank You, God, that You assure us that "the sufferings of this present time are not worthy to be compared with the glory which shall be revealed in us" (Romans 8:18 KJV). You encourage us to believe, and if we do, we will see Your glory. You tell us that the hope of Your calling is the hope of Your glory. I invite Your glory to be more fully manifest in my life today.

CREATING HOLISTIC PROSPERITY

 Relationships and Family: When you invite the glory of God to rest on you, your family will be drawn to you and will feel more comfortable around you as they feel the presence of God.

 Health: The glory of God is a place of peace and hope. Your emotions are automatically buffered against the harshness of the world, fears, and even reactive feelings that lead to negative consequences in your body.

 Financial: This chapter's opening verse says that the wealth of nations will come to you when you allow the glory of God to rest on you and you pursue the glory of God as well.

 Professional: The glory of God makes you more attractive to customers and opens more doors for employment.

Mindset: The glory of God has the power to change minds and hearts, to help you see options you did not see before, to see the redemption in every area.

 Social: The glory of God unites people. It helps them get along, work in unity, and bond together.

PART 3

Increasing Emotional and Physical Prosperity

God loves caring for and empowering the body and the soul. Through His Word, He reveals a desire to make humanity whole, healing emotions and bodies. His plan is that we would steward both our emotions and our bodies to be the most beautiful representation of Him. Emotional and physical health seem like two different things, but our emotions impact our bodies in powerful ways. Have you heard of someone being lovesick? Or feeling nervous knots in their stomach? Or feeling that something is a pain in the neck?

How we feel emotionally often manifests in our bodies. Emotional stress often leads to sickness or physical exhaustion. The Word of God says that a joyful heart is good medicine. The impact of joy and gratitude appear to strengthen our immune systems, decrease our blood pressure, and even reduce our feelings of physical pain. On the other hand, nutrition and exercise impact our moods, sometimes in dramatic ways. Our bodies and emotions are made in the image of God, we are living temples, and we are called to have prosperous temples.

15

Slow to Anger

*He who is slow to anger is better than the
    mighty,
And he who rules his spirit, than he who
    captures a city.*
—PROVERBS 16:32

The emotion of anger is not inherently good or bad. Anger is an emotion created by God to help motivate us to notice injustice or when something is wrong. It is not a "bad" emotion because God and Jesus both felt and expressed anger (Isaiah 30:27–28; Matthew 21:12–13; Mark 3:5). It is important to be able to be angry because when it is a godly response, it motivates us to correct things, to create justice, and to understand ourselves and others.

What is not good is if we are "quickly provoked" (Ecclesiastes 7:9 NIV). If we are quick to anger, we may jump to conclusions before we have time to examine our anger. Once we know why the anger is there, we may find that Scripture already gives us a next step to be at peace again (repent, forgive, correct, or heal). It is essential for our prosperity that we are slow to anger because then we can discover the next step, which may bring us healing or restoration.

On the other hand, if we just vent our anger immediately, we may behave in a way that does not help us to return to peace and actually prolongs our distress. We may go into fight-or-flight mode and destroy our relationships or cut short our progress. Worst of all, we may allow our anger to be directed at God and, instead of allowing God to help us resolve the anger, if we leave ourselves alone with its burden, it may destroy us.

Let's consider a scenario: You are driving on the infamously over-crowded Interstate 405 in Los Angeles twice a day for work. On a good day a five-mile stretch can easily be a drive of more than one hour in traffic, for various reasons. You have increasingly become stressed. You are thinking about the time you are missing out on with your family, being late to your nephew's birthday party, or missing a presentation in your evening class. Suddenly someone cuts you off and slams on the brakes. You can feel the stress flooding your body, your heart racing, your mind spinning. It is no surprise that you are feeling angry.

Instead of reacting to the message of anger, you remember Proverbs 16:32 and think, *I can rule these emotions!* You thank the anger for sending you a message. The feeling was unpleasant but rightfully so. The message is that you could have been hurt, and it is right to fear and feel anger about someone's actions possibly causing you harm. That feeling of anger is meant to motivate you to avoid harmful situations when possible and tell you that it is not good when others' actions cause you harm. You are no longer in danger of being hurt, and the situation is over. The message of anger is not the point. Your response to the message is.

Anger can come from failed expectations, betrayal, fear, rejection, loss, pain, exhaustion, and many other things. The feeling of anger should provoke us to set boundaries with ourselves to change our situations. We are not alone in this process of girding up our emotions. God Himself felt anger and had to control it. We are invited to steward our emotions well. When we recognize that the emotion we are feeling is big, we should put a plan in place instead of letting the emotion overtake us. This inner strength will make us unshakable in every season of adversity.

BUILDING YOUR PROSPEROUS EMOTIONAL AND PHYSICAL LIFE

Being slow to anger starts with awareness. What is a sign in your body that tells you that you are angry (upset stomach, headache, shaking, feeling hot, craving sweets)? These physical experiences are part of how God designed you to know your "mailbox is full" because of a message that anger is trying to send you. So what do you do next?

1. Recognize and write out the message anger sent so you can understand it without prejudging it as good or bad.
2. Soothe or comfort yourself in a healthy way. Accept God's compassion for the "angry you." Have an attitude of curiosity and kindness toward yourself and the message.
3. Process the message with God. Identify the fear, pain, confusion, loss, or threat that you feel. Ask God how you might resolve those core feelings. Through prayer? Through acceptance? Through change? Through conversation? How can you

create a productive and empowering resolution that honors
you, God, and others?

4. Is there any proactive step you can or should take right now?

PROSPERITY PRAYER

*Jesus, You have a technical right to be angry above anyone else.
You have faced bullying, physical abuse, loss, pain, betrayal, and
unjust death. You are my greatest resource in learning how and
when to express anger so that it empowers my future and helps me
bring things into the right order. Let me see beyond the veil of my
own understanding and receive the message my anger is providing,
without allowing the anger to rule over me or my life.*

CREATING HOLISTIC PROSPERITY

Relationships and Family: It is okay that family
brings out strong emotions. They are a big part of us and
a big part of what meets our needs in life. Strive to live
in the strength of being happy no matter what they do.

Spiritual: Resist the temptation to blame God for
the sake of trying to understand something that went
wrong. It may be the easy answer and an easy outlet for
anger, but it is not helpful, healthy, or adding strength
to you.

Financial: Remove yourself from the emotional experience of finances. Finances are math problems, and strong emotions tend to mess up our ability to solve math problems.

 Professional: Being slow to anger allows you to assess the actual problem and solve it, rather than being overwhelmed and stuck in fight-or-flight emotions. Law is logic free from passion.

 Mindset: Work for a mindset of maintaining the ability to problem solve, governing your emotional response enough to continue to do this in a healthy way at any time.

 Social: If you are strong in your ability to regulate your emotions, people will trust you more and you will be seen as a rock and pillar socially. Your relationships will be stronger and more secure.

16

Self-Control

Like a city whose walls are broken through
is a person who lacks self-control.
—PROVERBS 25:28 NIV

In the beginning Adam and Eve were presented with a multitude of options. They could go wherever, do whatever, and eat whatever. God did not stop them from roaming freely and making their own decisions. Why? Because He already gave them a gift. He gave them one of the most powerful gifts given to humanity: the ability to receive, harness, and self-regulate the multitude of options to cultivate the best-case scenario in their lives and surroundings.

Even before the first temptation, God introduced the first gift to Adam and Eve: self-control. He made sure His grace (empowerment) was sufficient for their temptation, and they had the power and authority to bring about His will when presented with other options. They were hardwired by God to have self-control, and so are we! We can extend this power into our health and other areas of our life. For example, we can have self-control with our emotions, allowing them to bring us health, direction, resolution, clarity, and life instead of destruction.

I (Ally) once struggled with self-control in the area of my emotions. I was not able to control the negative feelings I had about myself. I didn't realize it, but by not having control, I was actively being self-destructive. The worse I felt, the less I hoped things would go well. I resisted trying new things like making friends, and I became more isolated. I would often try to feel the negative emotions and rehearse them, thinking I was trying to solve them, but there was never a solution. This was a sign to me that I needed to learn to manage these emotions in a healthy way. We don't want our emotions to cut us off and lead us away from a good future. Unruled, negative emotions can damage our bodies and spirits.

I began to get control of these negative thoughts and feelings by distracting myself, laughing inside at the emotions, and thinking of them as annoying instead of true. I asked others to help me see myself as God sees me, and then I would write out the positive emotions that God wanted me to experience. Step-by-step I learned to stop dwelling on the negative. What God felt about me was the truth about who I really was. These new emotions about the person I really was were life giving. It wasn't easy, but gradually I built into myself the type of self-awareness God wanted me to have. It certainly has been more than worth it!

We can all grow in self-control like we grow our physical muscles through use, intention, support, and practice. It is a natural process that God has enacted as a gift. We can also advance in self-control through awareness, honesty with ourselves, and—my favorite way—delayed gratification. With delayed gratification, you don't reward yourself right away after an accomplishment. Delay the reward through planned self-control, and it will grow the power you have over your impulses and positive and negative motivations.

The Bible has a lot to say about self-control. In Proverbs 25:28, one without self-control is like a city with broken-down walls. That is a powerful picture of how we are to fortify ourselves with self-deployed control in order to thrive. If not, anything could get in to harm us. However, when we are fortified with patience and self-control, we become stronger than a warrior who takes an entire city (Proverbs 16:32). Nothing can stop us from becoming the best version of ourselves in our minds, bodies, and emotions.

BUILDING YOUR PROSPEROUS EMOTIONAL AND PHYSICAL LIFE

It is important to consider what makes you more vulnerable to losing control so you can make small course corrections throughout your day and week and not be overwhelmed later.

1. Consider an area where you feel you lack self-control. Shopping, eating, yelling, or any other area.
2. Make a list of things that make you vulnerable to losing self-control in that area. It could be exhaustion, something in the environment (for example, seeing sweets tends to lead to eating them), loneliness, disappointment, getting into a fight, being criticized at work, getting stuck in traffic, feeling disrespected, and so forth.
3. Each day check in about how your vulnerability factors are going. Give yourself space to emotionally reset and strengthen yourself with encouragement, connection, a spiritual practice, making a joke about it, or talking to a friend. Do this before you get past the point of maintaining self-control.

4. Think of your response as bringing you either further from prosperity or closer to it.

PROSPERITY PRAYER

God, You are the Author of our process, and You care more than we do about our success. Thank You for giving us the same gift that You gave Jesus—self-control. Help us to reach new depths in vulnerability with ourselves and the inner strength to empower Your will in our lives. You are the God of self-control. Nothing over-powers You. Teach us Your precious ways. Help us walk with the One we love.

CREATING HOLISTIC PROSPERITY

Relationships and Family: Have self-control in how you think of others, desire to gossip, or are tempted to shame others. Having an open mind and self-control with judgments and assumptions can greatly improve your relationships.

Spiritual: It is a gift from God! The amount of control we are willing to develop with Him indicates the amount of control we can walk in and the amount we can be entrusted with in life.

Financial: Emotional purchasing can destroy a financial plan. Use self-control to obtain long- and short-term goals with your friends.

Professional: Much of our success at work is not based on what we say; it is based on what we don't say. Enjoy self-control to maintain professional relationships.

 Mindset: Self-control demonstrates power. Power is revealed in restraint, not in abundance. Think with restrained thoughts, and practice restraining and having self-control with thoughts that don't serve God's purpose and plan for your life.

 Social: When making decisions, have self-control with your own desires and ask what would benefit you community, group, or church the most.

17

Restoration

So I will restore to you the years that the
      swarming locust has eaten,
The crawling locust,
The consuming locust,
And the chewing locust,
My great army which I sent among you.
You shall eat in plenty and be satisfied,
And praise the name of the LORD your God,
Who has dealt wondrously with you;
And My people shall never be put to
      shame.
      —JOEL 2:25–26 NKJV

Sometimes things don't go as planned. However, God is not surprised by this news. He is acquainted with the mystery of humanity. He created us! When things make a turn for the worse, we have the most amazing strategist in the history of the world helping us put them back together. When the breakdown begins, restoration is required to bring things back to life. When God restores something, it may not be the same as it once was, but it could be way better.

Jesus' ultimate job on the earth was to restore humanity back to the Father. Restoration is part of our natural design. We all strive to walk in the perfect will of God, but when we fall short, we can be surrounded with thoughts, feelings, and plans of restoration. When God restores, He makes it better than before. Remember Job? God restored to Job twice as much as he had lost. Consider Joel. God restored years of loss back to him. How good is God!

One area of restoration is in our health. Sometimes our bodies send us messages that we are not well. This could be physical pain, the onset of type 2 diabetes, problems with our skin, or other signs. God has given us natural processes to care for our bodies as we would care for a temple. By following doctors' advice and health advice, we can restore ourselves to be healthier than we have been in years! We can restore prosperity to our physical bodies.

When it comes to emotional health, we also get signs of how things are going when we are not doing well emotionally. How we respond to those signs determines our ability to overcome and recover. Job is a great example of this. Yes, he lost almost everything, but he did not allow his emotions to cause him to take actions that were more detrimental. He did not "curse God and die" as his wife so unhelpfully suggested (Job 2:9 NIV). That would have been an emotional reaction that was not helpful. Had he cursed God, he might never have seen the exceedingly abundant restoration God had for him.

We have all experienced loss and need restoration. I (Jeremy) went through seasons of loss. I lost some of the dearest people, and yet I have maintained one stance that has been the bedrock for my emotions to rest on: whenever I lost or felt loss, I remembered that

Jesus knew that loss and feeling. Jesus is the most relatable person. My suffering was not from God, and God had the ability to restore it because He understands it.

How we steward our emotions, hearts, minds, and relationships when things are lost is key to our restoration process. If we push them away, send blame, or shut down, it can be detrimental. God always has a plan for restoration. Will you allow your emotions to have enough peace so that you can hear His still, small voice lead you back to prosperity? God's redemptive will is part of your inheritance. Allow Him to restore the years of loss.

BUILDING YOUR PROSPEROUS EMOTIONAL AND PHYSICAL LIFE

The things we tell ourselves and the words we use are powerful. They can impact the long-term outcome and be a way we partner with God for redemption. Even if you don't fully believe it, this exercise could have a powerful impact on your brain, to open your mind and emotions to redemption.

1. Think of a situation of loss or lack in your life. Write out your thoughts about the situation.
2. Go through your writing and circle the words that are related to powerlessness, fear, anxiety, anger, or other emotions that could have a toxic effect if not resolved.
3. Ask God if your emotionally loaded words are the words He would use, or if your thoughts are causing you to assume redemption is not possible.
4. What would it look like for you to take a hard situation from the past and adjust those words into words that indicate redemption or empowerment?

PROSPERITY PRAYER

Jesus, You are a redemptive God. You give us plans of restoration, plans of love and repair for every area of loss, setback, or separation. Thank You for leading and guiding us into restoration. You care for us so well. We give You every emotion, thought, and mindset that keeps us from our best selves. Thank You for being there for us to bring us into Your redemptive plan.

CREATING HOLISTIC PROSPERITY

 Relationships and Family: Being open to restoration even when there is not full forgiveness or full resolution can open a door for continued growth in the relationship, even after challenges.

 Spiritual: The ultimate spiritual restoration occurred when Jesus died for your spiritual restoration. Walking this out daily can transform every area of life as you accept the death, burial, and resurrection of Jesus.

 Financial: If you are in debt or dealing with a financial loss, actively pursue opportunities to restore finances by receiving education (online or from trusted friends) about how to reduce debt.

 Professional: Be proactive to find ways to restore your working relationships. If there is a breach in trust or a challenging situation, be humble in seeking to restore and resolve the challenges and continue to work with the people involved, if possible.

Mindset: Reframe your current life and future as a restoration narrative of how God wants to restore all your past. Allow pain to be restored to hope.

 Social: One of the best ways to restore social divides is to see life through others' eyes in a way that brings healing and restoration to people groups and social groups.

18

Declaration

(As it is written, "A FATHER OF MANY NATIONS HAVE I MADE YOU") in the presence of Him whom he believed, even God, who gives life to the dead and calls into being that which does not exist.

—ROMANS 4:17

Communication is a core component to our daily exchanges. When we speak, we speak from a place of perspective, knowledge, and experience, which paves the way for reciprocity in life. There are so many ways to communicate, all of which accomplish different goals and outcomes. God delights in words. He created the heavens and the earth with His words. He is a huge fan of communication. God's words are so powerful they call into existence things that did not exist before. As we are made in His image, our words also have the same power to create.

God used His initial form of communication, declaration, to create the vast expanse we know and love today. Declarations are about calling forth the realized potential of a matter into the present tense from a place of authority. God spoke out loud what He saw in His heart and mind, and thus He created. Declarations work because the power of our words brings alignment to our hearts, minds, emotions, bodies, and especially health. Wherever we have alignment, we gain access to what is possible.

Declaration makes way for the mind to follow into the path of truth. When John the Baptist looked over the ridge and said, "Behold, the Lamb of God who takes away the sin of the world" (John 1:29), he was declaring the truth that was right in front of him. He saw it before anyone else did. John was able to rightly align himself with the word of truth, and he fulfilled what God called him to. When we declare, just like John, we open a way in our minds for the fulfillment of unrealized promises. We can declare over our places of need these available promises.

There are two main ways of operating in the world: from our heads or from our hearts. You may have heard it said, "Did that decision come from that person's head or from their heart?" It is called the "head or heart" way of operating, but the two choices should not be mutually exclusive. When we have communication between the heart and the head, there is an exchange of valuable perspectives. Most people struggle to declare things because they do not feel in their hearts that they are true. The irony is that what we speak, our hearts will follow. When we start to speak differently, it impacts how we feel. When we feel good, it impacts how we think. When we are thinking well, it impacts what we do. When we are speaking, feeling, and thinking differently, we start to access our true promise and potential.

I (Ally) once had a mentee who was struggling with feeling unattractive. She felt her weight was holding her back from an abundant life. I encouraged her to start declaring what God said, that she was made in the image of God. Any judgments besides God's (even her own) could never be fully true, or as important as God's thoughts. I invited her to declare that the way she looked would not hold her back from life, love, or opportunity because all those things come from God. And I encouraged her to declare that she would have an abundant life and a body that helped her achieve the things she wanted to achieve in life.

At first, the young woman found this difficult because she did not believe she was worthy. We have the power, however, to tell our brains what to think. But as she started making these positive declarations, she began to focus on gratitude for the body she had, which led her to enjoy her life more fully. Her body naturally came into alignment with the truth, and—without dieting or striving—her body became more and more healthy. Instead of thinking of food as bad or a struggle, she started to think of food choices as something that added to or stole from an abundant life. This naturally guided her toward health. Her actions and thinking changed only because she started to declare the truth. The same can be true for you in any area you would like to change. Take action, declare the promises of God over your life today, and keep your head and heart in a prosperous relationship.

BUILDING YOUR PROSPEROUS EMOTIONAL AND PHYSICAL LIFE

Identify an area of emotional or physical health you want but have not yet achieved. It should focus around creating good habits—such as eating more natural, whole foods or having more peace. It should not focus on trying to stop doing something—such as eating fewer processed foods or feeling less stressed. We are more motivated when we frame things as trying to get what we want instead of avoiding something we feel bad about doing.

1. Thank God that He created you to live an abundant life. Thank Him that He gave you the power to increase that abundance through partnership.
2. Declare God's perspective on your health. Focus on His vision for you, not on how you might feel that you have failed. Use "I" statements (for example, "I am thankful I have the authority to be at peace").
3. Ask for wisdom from others who have achieved your health goals.
4. Read motivational quotes or stories about people who have achieved your goals.
5. Declare their wisdom over yourself as well.
6. Send yourself a notification or appointment on your phone to remind you.

PROSPERITY PRAYER

Lord, just as You place a banner over me, I declare that every cell of my body will be in proper alignment and health. I ask You to bring to remembrance the promises You have for me and help my declarations bring glory to You. Align my words to cocreate with You and bring about Your truth in my life and into the earth. Thank You for Your continued love, Jesus.

CREATING HOLISTIC PROSPERITY

 Relationships and Family: In conversations, declaring the best over someone helps actively empower them to become who they were created to be, and it helps them feel known and cared for, which increases the likelihood they will care for you.

Spiritual: Declaring changes the spiritual atmosphere to release the thing declared. If you can see something that is possible in the heart of God and speak it into existence, you are partnering with the God who spoke the world into existence.

 Financial: Declare life and prosperity over your finances by speaking God's promises. God spoke all things into existence, including resources. He has no shortage for you.

 Professional: Declare those things that are not as though they are. The goal is that it makes a road map for where you are heading and where God is bringing you so you can accept where things are going and where you are headed.

 Mindset: Declare mindsets that are biblical, but that you do not yet have, to bring them into reality. If you can speak it, you can imagine it; if you can imagine it, you can dream it; if you can dream it, you can live it.

 Social: Declare life and prosperity over your region to bring hope and ideas that motivate change.

19

Dying to a Matter

That which you sow does not come to life unless it dies.

—1 Corinthians 15:36

While building a new structure can help us get into our new season, alternatively, we may need to die to a matter to position ourselves for new life. A popular song came out a few years ago, and the main chorus says, "Let it go, let it go; can't hold it back anymore." Sometimes we need to just let it go. The apostle Paul talked about dying daily so that he could be raised in the newness of life (1 Corinthians 15:31; Romans 6:4). This is also true in our emotions and negative health habits. God's great grace and mercy is new daily. We are called to die daily to live by the sufficiency of God's grace.

Dying to a matter increases accurate receptivity to ourselves and to God. It gives us permission to reset our emotions and accept grace.

One of the most freeing things is to die to the belief that others' reactions, emotions, and thoughts are about us. This may sound simple, but its complexity is often overlooked. I (Ally) used to struggle with taking things personally. Every comment and look was interpreted as a coded message about me. The message was always negative. On the one hand, it is good to be aware of what others might feel or think, but we shouldn't live our lives assuming negative judgments about us are being made or are true.

I gained tremendous freedom when I died to the desire to know and control what others thought about me. I died to the bad habit of trying to know others' thoughts. I died to the constant wondering if others (including myself) thought I was good enough, smart enough, social enough, and so forth. I died to the right to judge myself. As I did this, I was empowered to come back to life in new ways. I allowed Jesus to have power over this part of my thought life. I then started to live with the assumption that others thought the same about me that Jesus did. If they didn't, that was information about them, not me.

Dead people cannot take anything personally. If we live in our own strength, we will need to support ourselves. However, if we die with Him, we will also be raised with Him (Romans 6:8). This is true in so many ways with negative emotions and habits. Many of the habits that negatively impact our bodies are things we have not died to. We think we have to take our thoughts and feelings as our full truth. It is important to both accept our thoughts and feelings and allow God to show us where we are making our lives miserable by not dying to a matter. We will prosper more when we die to thoughts that don't help us. Let go of emotions and fears that diminish our lives and are not helping us live according to our values and goals.

Humility and hope will guide us when we let go. God will make something good out of what we let go of. Let's be willing to let go so we can enter into the divine exchange. Sometimes it can be intentional that we die to something, and sometimes we might not have a choice or feel we have a choice. But either way, dying to a matter, like experiencing a loss, allows a seed of life, light, and truth to be planted where it can grow strongly. Have an honest conversation with God and yourself about things you need to let go of. God is faithful to comfort you. He wants to see you in the newness of life that He has always planned for you.

BUILDING YOUR PROSPEROUS EMOTIONAL AND PHYSICAL LIFE

Today practice a way of dying to yourself so that the new creation can be reborn! Here are actions to choose from:

- Die to the desire to be right. Those who have a strong need to be right often miss important things in life, which creates barriers to prosperity. Sometimes this need brings more damage than good. Replace the desire to be right with the willingness to be curious.
- Die to the belief that other people's reactions, thoughts, expressions, and interactions with you are about you. People react only how they allow themselves to, and each person is fully responsible for his or her deeds and emotional reactions. Practice taking responsibility for yours, and your mindset will shift.
- Die to the belief that you can or should control others or make them think or do anything. Instead, practice sharing your thoughts, ideas, and process in conversation, and let others make their own decisions.

PROSPERITY PRAYER

Jesus, I see You show me the way to thrive, and I see that thriving is about leaving behind what is not prospering and pursuing what is. I give all things into Your hands and die to what is not good for me so that I have the chance to fully live in You. You are my strength and my Rock. I choose to be raised in the newness of life with You!

CREATING HOLISTIC PROSPERITY

Relationships and Family: Die to who you want your family members to be, or who you think they should be, and allow yourself to discover and empower them for who they actually are.

Spiritual: "Hope deferred makes the heart sick" (Proverbs 13:12). Better to die to hope for some things so your heart is not sick and you can be free. Trust God to bring the hope back to life if He desires and if it is best for you. Then you know it is not coming out of your own strength.

Financial: When investments and purchases don't go well, allow the hope of salvaging things to die. Detach emotions from the math problem at hand and shut investments down before they become more destructive.

Professional: Not every product, client, or service will go well. To move from strength to strength you have to let it go and not dwell on the loss or setback so much that it poisons the deal. Don't hang out with a dead deal.

Mindset: Let go of offense and things that don't go your way. Analyze unfruitful and painful memories to see if ruminating on them benefits your life or steals from it. Forgive others if needed, forgive yourself if needed, and move on.

 Social: Let your ego focus on solving problems, not on being right. Die to thinking you know the best way for your community and learn from your community what they need.

20

Diligence

Poor is he who works with a negligent hand,
But the hand of the diligent makes rich.
—PROVERBS 10:4

If we carry the posture and action of being diligent, we will reach abundance in all that we do. Why? Because diligence is a lifestyle that produces great results. We are not typically born diligent. Yes, there may be some variations based on personality, but by and large diligence is something we practice and can grow in throughout life. It is like a muscle, and as you work it out and build it, you can realize potential more and more every day. You push the barriers of possibility for what you are willing to withstand and what your capacity could be.

Diligence is universal. Whatever you are diligent toward in one area can be applied to others. We see this trait in athletes who diligently train their bodies, minds, and emotions to reach peak performances. Sports psychology is an entire field dedicated to understanding how the mind and emotions impact and potentially improve or impair performance.

I (Jeremy) spent time working on my "mental game" in sports when we were younger. I was a wrestler and played football. I practiced the art of diligence in training and worked to become the best at my craft. My high school football and wrestling teams both won the state championships three years in a row. The football team once held the third-best record in the nation as an undefeated high school team at forty-eight straight wins.

A hallmark of diligence is not giving up when things get hard or do not go as planned. For athletes, there can be many days of practice that do not go well. The key is that athletes continue to diligently look for ways to improve themselves.

If we think in terms of one decision, we won't make progress. If we think in terms of instantly getting our ultimate result, we also will stop making progress. We need to train ourselves not to run away or give up or change our goal just because we have a hard or less successful day. Changing goals too often creates an abortion of goals and discouragement or disappointment.

We must make sustained decisions and adjust to a new life with those decisions until they become habits. Day after day, week after week. These could be habits for your health or emotions. Yes! You can create emotional habits and have emotional hygiene each day. It demonstrates diligence to check in with your emotions and set goals for emotional stability and strength.

We may start to become diligent with what we put in our bodies. One key is to think in terms of what we are gaining, not losing. By being diligent to let go of grudges, we free our emotional space to gain peace and health. By saying no to junk food, we gain physical strength, stamina, and possibly a longer, more prosperous future. Diligence is an invitation to usher in prosperity. The hand of the diligent is rich. The power to step into emotional, physical, and mental health is through diligence.

BUILDING YOUR PROSPEROUS EMOTIONAL AND PHYSICAL LIFE

Certain emotions lead to thoughts that weaken you and move you away from the life God has for you. Others strengthen you and lead you toward the life God has for you.

- Create a schedule to help you remember to be diligent at checking in with your emotions once a day.
- Write for two to three minutes about anything that is bothering you or anything that is strengthening you and your emotional fortitude.
- Be diligent to accept and then resolve emotions through praying, talking to a friend, or reading Bible verses that speak truth over you. Do not let uncomfortable emotions continue to build unchecked and unresolved, or they will overwhelm you, creating negative behaviors or actions.
- Try letting go of unhelpful emotions in a symbolic way, such as writing them down and throwing away the paper or—Ally's favorite—putting the paper in a box labeled "Surrendered to God."

PROSPERITY PRAYER

Your diligence reveals to me Your love and care for me. Help me to model my life after You. Reveal the world of opportunity that is available to me when I work with all my heart toward the things You have for me. Show me how to press in and run after the goals that You have for me. I want to learn the diligence of Your love. Bless You, Jesus.

CREATING HOLISTIC PROSPERITY

 Relationships and Family: Diligently working toward communication skills, and skills that help others feel truly heard and understood, will help your friends and family open up more and will build trust between you.

 Spiritual: Be diligent to pursue the fruit of the Spirit. Make time and space and a plan to choose how you will live out the fruit of the Spirit, such as love, joy, peace, and so forth (Galatians 5:22–23).

 Financial: Be diligent to track spending, review receipts and bank statements for errors, and bring correction or proactive change if needed.

 Professional: Be diligent to watch over the quality of your work and deliver the best product possible.

Mindset: Be diligent to take inventory of your thoughts. Ask God if there are more helpful thoughts to replace the ones you have, thoughts to create a thriving life in your mind. Align with God, even when you don't feel like it.

 Social: Be diligent to watch over your purchases to see if they benefit or hurt communities and the world. Start to think about purchasing clothes, gifts, and household items that benefit those less fortunate and are fair trade and sustainable for the earth.

21

Asking

But if any of you lacks wisdom, let him ask of God, who gives to all generously and without reproach, and it will be given to him. But he must ask in faith without any doubting, for the one who doubts is like the surf of the sea, driven and tossed by the wind. For that man ought not to expect that he will receive anything from the Lord, being a double-minded man, unstable in all his ways.

—JAMES 1:5-8

A crippled man once came to Peter asking for money. Peter said he did not have money, but he proclaimed healing over the man, who then got up and walked. This miracle was only possible in the middle of the ask. Asking is simple, but it is key to unlocking the possibilities of the moment. Let's dive into the process of asking so we can unlock its rewards.

Asking is not a passive process; it involves clear steps. It is a powerful way to prosper. First, identify what you need and what others have. For someone to let down their guard and humbly inquire for information, understanding, or help is one of the easiest and simplest ways to prosperity. We are wired to help one another, and impartation and assistance is sometimes given for free by simply asking when others would be paying for the same type of help. Asking is an avenue of access where one's process can be opened up to transfer the very thing that is needed. Asking requires a partnership and follow-through to see fulfillment.

Second, ask in the right timing. Sometimes God withholds what we ask for because it is not the right time or season or because we couldn't handle the outcome if we got it. In the above scripture, however, it appears that a person's heart can get in the way of receiving. The verses do not say that God withholds giving. They say that the person does not receive it. Sometimes, that lack of receiving also has to do with doubt. It is the same way the Jews prayed for a Savior, had Him right in front of them, but did not receive Him. Our hearts and emotions can prevent us from having our asking fulfilled.

The final step is, then, to receive. Our emotions, mindsets, and situations can prevent us from receiving. Consider James 4:2, which says, "You desire but do not have, so you kill. You covet but you cannot get what you want, so you quarrel and fight. You do not have because you do not ask God" (NIV). Many times the answer is delayed because we are afraid. Yes, asking opens you up to vulnerable feelings.

Asking also helps create understanding that leads to peaceful and empowered emotions. When we are worried, confused, or afraid, asking can bring clarity. Ask, "Can you please help me understand what you mean when you say that?" or "What do you think is going on?" It can also help us to ask for what we need to have a better environment. For example, "The volume of the TV is giving me a headache. Do you mind if we turn it down?" This opens up the possibility to receive the truth of another's heart and intention. Asking can take us from good health to optimal health.

When it comes to our emotions, we can ask for help to understand our emotions, needs, and desires. If we do not communicate, others will not know. Often, asking is misunderstood as being weak. But it is a true way God has called us to prosper, and we have to be careful to not let pride or fear get in the way. God wants us to ask for things. We should partner with this amazing tool to ask away into the future seasons of life. Asking brings the inheritance of the listener to your fingertips.

BUILDING YOUR PROSPEROUS EMOTIONAL AND PHYSICAL LIFE

Sometimes we may ask too much, sometimes too little. Asking is about balance. Here are questions to help you consider if you should ask for something:

1. Do you know for sure that what you want is possible for the other person to give?
2. Have you already asked many things from this person without helping them or offering much in return?
3. How will you feel after asking? Will you feel proud and satisfied, or angry, or discouraged? How will you feel if the answer is no? If you would resent the answer, it may be best for the relationship that you do not ask.

4. Will your relationship have the chance to grow closer from the ask? Will the ask help build trust and healthy relational vulnerability?

5. Are there other ways to get your needs met? One of the biggest problems when asking is that we ask the first person who comes to our mind, and if we don't have backup plans, it can seem that we are desperate.

6. Are there potential consequences if you do not ask?

PROSPERITY PRAYER

The biggest invitation goes out from my heart and mind to You. You have presented me with a door made possible in every area of my life: my relations, my spiritual walk, my business, and my family. You have given me tools and a mindset and an application to open up that door. The key to what You have for me is asking. I know it is simple, but You open up this door in my heart. So I do not hide in my own thoughts and process, I invite You in, and I respond to what You have for me by asking for the greater, for the abundance of what is hidden in You. Humble me so I do not distain simple dependence and interdependence, and so I can ask.

CREATING HOLISTIC PROSPERITY

 Relationships and Family: Ask for help from family. When you do, they feel closer to you, feel like they value you more, and feel like you value them as well. It also gives them permission to ask from you.

Spiritual: Take the time to ask for God's thoughts, perspective, and interventions in a situation.

 Financial: Ask for help with strategic process, budgeting, and making sound financial plans.

 Professional: Ask for insight into how to do your job and grow your career. This will give you favor with your bosses or managers.

 Mindset: Instead of considering yourself an expert, keep asking, learning, growing, and being curious.

 Social: A great way to invite change and maintain connections in your social circles is by inquiring, being curious, and asking questions about things that are not going well in your community or things you would like from your community.

PART 4

Increasing Financial Prosperity

God cares about your finances. That is why He spent so much time talking about money. He was not scared of it. He was not scared to have it or not have it. In fact, fear of having or not having money did not drive Jesus to action on any occasion. Yet it was a very important topic to Him. Consider how many of the parables Jesus taught involved money. We have found that many people are afraid and ashamed about money, but that is not God's calling! We cannot ignore His big-picture plan for us. Nor can we assume He is responsible for our finances more than we are. He gave Adam resources in the garden to steward, and He gives us resources to steward today. Building a financial plan that cultivates legacy is the hallmark of a financially prospering Christian. God is eternal, and we believe His plan for our stewardship has eternal aspects. Money is a great resource to bring about transformation and good in our world.

22

Spouse

An excellent wife, who can find?
For her worth is far above jewels.
The heart of her husband trusts in her,
And he will have no lack of gain.
—PROVERBS 31:10-11

E very day people get married for love because love is the ultimate conduit for all relationships! Within love, couples can also
find purpose, which is essentially love walked out. When purpose
is engaged in a relationship, sparks begin to fly, dreams come alive,
businesses are birthed, and plans are formed. The unity of marriage
is built around purpose, action, and productivity. God first spoke and
said, "It is not good for the man to be alone; I will make him a helper

suitable for him" (Genesis 2:18). A helper to be fruitful and multiply with. This fruitfulness is beyond just having kids. It is a multiplication in every area of life—work, play, relationships, body, mind, and especially our finances.

Have you ever considered that your spouse could be the single greatest financial asset you will ever have? Allow me to explain. The proximity of a spouse to the deep and intimate avenues of one's life is unmatched by anyone else. They have access to the secrets, dreams, and desires of our hearts. If those secrets, dreams, and desires are nurtured correctly, prosperity will begin to abound. In Proverbs 31:11 above, we see this divine invitation. "The heart of her husband trusts in her, and he will have no lack of gain."

Imagine all the things an equally yoked couple can create. There are many obvious ways one can partner with their spouse for financial prosperity like building a business, filing jointly as a married couple for tax savings, and sharing assets. Let's look at a few not-so-obvious ways.

Your spouse can be your on-call emotional support system so you can perform at 100 percent in life. They can provide you with a built-in, trusted second opinion when making important decisions. One of my favorite ways for a spouse to help bring financial prosperity is the invisible multiplication factor that God endorses through partnership.

When I met Ally, I knew she would be easy to love and I was excited to enter into a season of mutually exchanging that love. Early in the relationship I realized I could love her and also fulfill my purpose and plans with her. This was an incredible revelation. Our connection provided the bedrock for our dreams to reach full term. Ally would often tell me that I should start consulting because she saw me helping others this way and that I was good at it. With her encouragement and support we started our company called Radiant

Thoughts, where we provide consulting services to writers and ministries. We were able to give birth to a company that has grown beyond our dreams.

Your spouse is your number-one teammate, not your competition. If you let them into your process through honesty, vulnerability, and intentionality, they can come alongside you, perfect your strengths, and cover your weaknesses. Through this deep connection, trust can abound in your financial foundation. A mission, vision, and values can be established in the relationship in perpetuity, which will give a clarion call to every small purchase and every big investment a couple should make.

When you became one and God unified you and your spouse on your wedding day, He unified the purpose and potential that you have with your partner. A new vision was brought forth, and with a new vision comes new provision. It's time to discover the possibility of this new season! Explore ways for you to grow in your connection with your spouse and new streams of life and income will surface.

BUILDING YOUR PROSPEROUS FINANCIAL LIFE

If you are married, consider scheduling a financial planning meeting with your spouse. If you want to be married, consider the financial situation you can work toward at the beginning of the marriage. If you don't plan to be married, consider the financial future you want to create for yourself. Start by asking yourself these questions:

- What is your financial mission? What has God called you to do with your finances? What will you be proud of doing with your finances in the next five years?

- What is your financial vision? What do you foresee happening with your income, with bonuses, and with big purchases during the next five years? How can you plan for this?
- What are your values for your finances? Are you spending accordingly? Create a hierarchy of things that you value and things you don't to help guide your purchasing.

PROSPERITY PRAYER

God, You know the dreams and desires of my heart. You also know the dreams and desires of my spouse's heart. I invite You into our process and allow You to do wonderous things in our lives. We bless You, Jesus, for Your plan that You set forth in the garden that we can feel in our bones. Thank You for Your display of fruitful connections and how they produce so much throughout the Bible. Guide us, Jesus, into new ways of financial prosperity in this season. We will follow You.

CREATING HOLISTIC PROSPERITY

 Relationships and Family: Your marriage provides the opportunity to build and grow from a trusted relational perspective.

 Spiritual: Embrace the multiplication factor, where God blesses the unity and collaboration of marriage relationship.

Health: Processing emotions and experiences within your relationship will provide perspective and decrease loneliness.

 Professional: Speaking truth and potential into your dreams will help you process, plan, and think about how to deal with professional issues.

 Mindset: Knowing you have a partner in all that you do, one who supports you unconditionally, gives you a reality check and helps you see yourself as Christ sees you. This is especially important when you are having discouraging thoughts about yourself. And you can be that partner for your spouse.

 Social: Expand your social network through your spouse and you may bring balance to your relationships (for example, when one spouse is more outgoing and extroverted and the other is more introverted).

23

Humility

By humility and the fear of the LORD
Are riches and honor and life.
—PROVERBS 22:4 NKJV

Humility is often misunderstood. Most think of it as modesty or meekness or, in other words, apologizing often. During my doctoral studies, I (Ally) took an independent study class on humility and how it impacts leaders and leadership, businesses, and therapy. From the perspective of psychology, one definition of humility is that it is about having an accurate view of yourself. It is about understanding your strengths and weaknesses enough to properly convey them. Humility is not about downplaying or pretending you don't have strengths. It is the true reflection of one's self. When someone gives the most authentic representation of who they are and what they are about, they display humility.

False humility is shown by resisting giving help or advice and by keeping quiet and being reserved. Under the guise of humility, people sometimes don't offer advice that could help or they don't teach on a subject they know a lot about. Humility is not about hiding the truth. It is about being more vulnerable and authentic. It is also not overestimating your strengths or acting like you have no weaknesses. In fact, having an accurate view of your strengths and weaknesses enables you to be more relatable to those around you. In Proverbs 22:4 above, we see that humility coupled with the fear of the Lord creates a path for abundance. Not just any abundance but riches and honor and life! Humility is the secret to a great life.

How does humility apply financially? My (Jeremy's) sister-in-law Samantha is a great example. She has an accurate view of her finances and is willing to find money-saving opportunities when she can. One way she does this is through couponing. She loves the process, and even though she does not have to use coupons, she finds joy in it and finds it to be a way she can gain more financial prosperity for her family. She is not so prideful that she feels couponing is beneath her, even though some in her same financial situation might feel that way. She does not cut off financial prosperity for fear of the judgment of others.

We have a friend who is a real estate agent and broker. She has gained a reputation for giving people an accurate view of what they can afford. Often she will talk a buyer out of buying a more expensive house. She could convince them to buy it and receive a bigger commission herself, but instead she gives them an accurate assessment. Many people come back and thank her for convincing them not to buy their dream house because they later fell on hard times or didn't realize how much the house upkeep would cost. This causes our friend to get return clients and many referrals because she is trustworthy. Financial humility is better than getting a dream home. Sadly, many people do not have this honest input. We have seen many people fall into emotional, relational, financial, and spiritual destruction because they bought a house they could not afford and then waste years of their lives under the financial pressure and stress.

Financial humility involves getting out of the paycheck-to-paycheck mentality by having an accurate view of your finances and an accurate view of life. Sometimes people spend more than they can afford and have an unrealistic view of what they should buy. Financial humility provides longevity in financial infrastructure. It helps you build a future. Financial humility is thinking ten years out and thinking about finances long term, not just in the moment. You are not trying to paint an accurate view of yourself when you are trying to prove something to others by how you spend what you have or by the house you live in.

When we submit our finances to God, we are entering into humility. Through our honesty and vulnerability, we will find true stewardship and responsibility. Financial humility is about abiding in the contentment of today while building the goals of tomorrow. We can all do this! Be true to yourself and communicate that truth into your finances and walk it out, knowing God is on your side.

BUILDING YOUR PROSPEROUS FINANCIAL LIFE

Think of one thing you bought during the last month that might have been outside your means, maybe something that you now realize you don't need, want, get much benefit from, or something that took you further from your financial goals. Ask yourself these questions:

- What drove you to buy it? Was it for convenience? Was it something you bought to feel better in the moment? Was it something you bought out of guilt or because you were trying to impress someone?
- Whatever need, emotion, or want triggers your overspending, start to look for creative ways to fill that need. For example, practicing gratitude for five minutes before making a purchase boosts your mood so you do not rely on the purchase to do that.
- Find an accountability partner to help remind you of the deeper needs you need to be vigilant to satisfy so that you do not succumb to emotional purchasing.

PROSPERITY PRAYER

Jesus, who is more authentic than You? You lead and guide us into a true reflection of ourselves. We love humility because it brings us closer to You. You are a humble God who is real and honest with us. Thank You, Jesus, for being a perfect representation of the Father. We want to be like You. Help us to not fake it anymore but to just be ourselves. Thank You, Jesus, for Your strength in this. We love You.

CREATING HOLISTIC PROSPERITY

 Relationships and Family: Having an accurate assessment of who you are and conveying that to those around you will advance you in the stages of life. Overestimating or underestimating yourself will hurt your relationships and connection potential.

Spiritual: Develop an accurate understanding of your strengths and abilities, what you can give, who you are, and what your spiritual gifts are. As you do this, you will know what you can offer. This builds the healthiest bridge for people to engage with you.

 Health: Be willing to accept that your body and emotions need help at times. If you do not pursue and accept help, you will end up hurting yourself. Unless you are an expert physician or psychologist, don't assume you know when you need help. Don't let your pride get in the way of long-term success.

 Professional: As a leader, communicate and learn to laugh at and share your weaknesses as much—if not more—than your strengths. This allows your team to feel free to do the same and the company not to be run by people who feel pressure to fake things they don't actually know.

 Mindset: Do not succumb to pressure to pretend that you have gifts you do not. Be happy to learn and grow from the gifts and skills of others, while knowing what you are competent in and what you are not.

 Social: Learn what the needs of others are. Lead with serving others by meeting their needs, not simply sharing your gifts. If you see your strengths as a means to serve, you will always be rightly positioned for connection and growth.

24

Creative Ingenuity

Then Jacob took fresh rods of poplar and almond
and plane trees, and peeled white stripes in
them, exposing the white which was in the rods.
—Genesis 30:37

Jacob's interesting story continues:

He set the rods which he had peeled in front of the flocks in the gutters, even in the watering troughs, where the flocks came to drink;
and they mated when they came to drink. So the flocks mated by
the rods, and the flocks brought forth striped, speckled, and spot-
ted. Jacob separated the lambs, and made the flocks face toward the
striped and all the black in the flock of Laban; and he put his own
herds apart, and did not put them with Laban's flock. Moreover,
whenever the stronger of the flock were mating, Jacob would place

the rods in the sight of the flock in the gutters, so that they might mate by the rods; but when the flock was feeble, he did not put them in; so the feebler were Laban's and the stronger Jacob's. So the man became exceedingly prosperous, and had large flocks and female and male servants and camels and donkeys. (Genesis 30: 38–43)

The innovator in all of us comes alive when we have goals and we partner with God's creativity to bring them about. God first revealed Himself as the Creator. Creative ingenuity is God's middle name. He made us out of dust and breathed life into us. Furthermore, we are made in His image, and we have creativity flowing through our veins. We simply need to partner our creativity to our finances, and whole worlds of prosperity will open up.

We are set free the day we realize our money comes from God. He holds the keys to our financial future. Sure, we partner with people today, and they provide avenues of financial prosperity for our time or services. But those opportunities come out of God's grace and our partnership. If this is true, then we can create new ways of financial prosperity. We can be innovative with our current revenue streams to maximize our returns by thinking outside of the box.

Ethics aside, Jacob certainly had a unique idea to increase his flock, and he found a way to implement it. Wow, he was creative and exceedingly prosperous! One of my favorite modern-day stories about creative ingenuity is the story of the Michelin star restaurant guide. In 1900, the Michelin tire company wanted to encourage people to drive more so tires would need to be replaced more often and Michelin would make more money. They also wanted to connect car travel with luxury travel and convince more people to buy cars, therefore increasing the demand for tires. At the time, other guidebooks expected people to travel by train.

Michelin started to publish an annual guidebook of the best hotels and restaurants, awarding them "Michelin stars" based on the quality. The guidebook also contained maps, tips on how to care for your Michelin tires, advertisements, where to find gas along the way (there were no gas stations back then), where to find repair shops, and more. Michelin focused on locations spread around the country to allow people to "tour" (aka travel farther by car). This helped their primary business and created new ones. They are still around today, more than one hundred years later, as both a leading tire manufacturer and a restaurant guide.

Cambridge English Dictionary defines *ingenuity* as "someone's ability to think of smart new ways of doing something."[3] The Michelin brothers and Jacob in the Bible had creative and clever ways to increase their financial standing. We can all think creatively about how to meet people's needs or improve their lives. Find a need and start to dream. We applaud companies that innovate to solve problems, such as Wag (an app-based walker for your pets when you are away from home), Instacart (grocery home delivery from almost any store), and Amazon (one-day shipping on almost anything).

When we set financial goals, it gives us a target to pray into, dream about, and get creative with. Then we take our goals and match them with the problems we are trying to solve or the services we are trying to provide. God wants to share His creative solutions with us every day. As we simply invite Him into our minds, our processes, and our dreams, we will partner His creativity with our financial needs He already knows we have. The key is to not complain about them but find ways to partner with Him.

BUILDING YOUR PROSPEROUS FINANCIAL LIFE

Think of a goal and practice opening your mind to innovative ways to reach it. We often try to predict how to achieve things based on how things worked in the past. But the world, its people, and our experiences are always changing. It is important to get as much information as possible first. If you are stuck, try these tips:

1. Start by setting a goal.
2. List ways you have tried in the past to achieve that same goal or a similar one.
3. Find seven new, creative ways to reach that goal. Don't worry too much about practicality or ability at this point.
4. If you get stuck, ask your friends and family about creative ways to achieve that goal and how they have reached their goals, or google or watch YouTube videos about how others achieved that goal.

PROSPERITY PRAYER

God, we delight in Your clever, creative ways. Help us see the world from Your perspective. We look to You for creative strategies to solve all our financial needs. You know the ways that will unlock our prosperity. We listen and look to You. Thank You for always blessing us with Your wisdom, ingenuity, and love.

CREATING HOLISTIC PROSPERITY

 Relationships and Family: Think creatively about the places, situations, conversations, and activities that bring out the best in your family and relationships. Focus on those things when you spend time together.

Spiritual: God is the most creative force on the planet. He has creative thoughts and solutions that are outside our minds, but if we pursue His mind, we can see them too. Do not limit God. He has made water come from a rock and the Red Sea part. Be open to any way God can work.

 Health: There are creative ways to integrate physical health into your daily life. Change junk food for fruit or veggies, go window shopping for exercise. If cleared by your doctor, find creative ways to add five minutes of exercise at a time to feel better emotionally and physically.

 Professional: Always be willing to change and innovate before the customer or your boss asks you to. Surprise them with creative bonuses, initiatives, and ideas for how to make their experience better.

 Mindset: Have the mindset that there are twelve ways to tackle any problem. This brings freedom and peace and hope. There is a way—you just might not have found it yet. Creative thinking is like a muscle; the more you use it, the stronger it gets.

 Social: Challenge yourself to get over your fear of disconnection and be willing to try new things and join new groups by yourself.

25

Discernment

*But the Pharisees went out and conspired
against Him, as to how they might destroy Him.
But Jesus, aware of this, withdrew from there.
Many followed Him, and He healed them all.*

—MATTHEW 12:14–15

There are twenty-three hundred verses on finances in the Bible. Jesus spent more than 15 percent of His time talking about money because He knew how vital our finances are. How do we know what to do with our money? The world provides us with a million things we can spend our money on. We may want to purchase a house or car or go out to dinner. How do we know how much we can spend? When we are at work and we are signing a contract for a venue rental, how do we know if it's a good deal? Natural and spiritual discernment is the answer!

There was once a guy who watched every episode of the TV show *The Price Is Right*. Then one magical day he became a contestant on the show. He had studied the prices so much, he was able to guess perfectly all the way through and win the grand prize. He was so flawless in his guesses that the producers of the show thought someone had cheated and given him the answers. They were confused because this had never happened before. But the man had practiced his natural discernment enough to read the situation and recall the best answers.[4]

Discernment is a gift from God that helps us analyze a situation. We get raw data with our natural and spiritual discernment. It can be good data or bad data. It's up to us to interpret and make use of it. When Jesus said, "Walk into the room and let your peace go out from you. If it is not received, take it back in" (Matthew 10:13, our paraphrase), that is discernment in action. You let your peace go out. No one is willing to receive it, so you take it back. In another analogy, you start a conversation with your friends to share great news, but you feel unsettled inside about telling them, so you wait and move on. Discernment can be a feeling, impression, notion, or thought.

Discernment coupled with finances is incredible. We become great at reading people for negotiations, sales, and discounts. We can assess the true cost of something outside all the hoopla and gimmicks. In Matthew 25:14–30, the parable of the talents shows us how the first two servants used discernment on what to do with their money. They realized their moment of visitation, and they ran with it. God, of course, blessed them with amazing financial returns.

I (Jeremy) have worked hard to cultivate discernment. I can price anything! Ally frequently tests me on this. She likes to think it helps me to grow my gift, so she will quiz me on what things are worth, from castles to houses to the daily operational budget of one Disney park. I sometimes book venues for work. I was recently in a venue negotiation with one of the more expensive locations in town. I started talking to their event department and felt I could secure the venue for at least ten thousand dollars less than the asking price. Sure enough, I was able to do this thanks to emotional intelligence and discernment.

Discernment allows us to see beyond the surfaces to the heart of a matter. Does something feel off? Are the numbers telling the truth? Is something more promising? Is this a good opportunity? Naturally and spiritually we can grow in this gift. We can use discernment for all our financial decisions: hiring, purchasing, negotiating, selling, and interpreting a person or situation. Discernment is powerful. We should use this gift as often as we can to give us the best information to propel our financial life.

BUILDING YOUR PROSPEROUS FINANCIAL LIFE

Discernment is a way that we can measure the natural and spiritual environments. We should use it to upgrade our ability to measure good investments, purchases, and deals. If the deal looks great on paper but your discernment is telling you otherwise, then it could be a great resource to save you from losing a lot of money. Here are a few ways you can incorporate discernment into your finances:

1. Take an assessment of your thoughts, emotions, and feelings before you enter a conversation or negotiation. Receive and understand the message from your emotions and feelings. If you are picking up on things that are not directly communicated, this may be helpful in your decision process.
2. Present your plan to God and inquire about His response.
3. Sleep on it! Do not rush big decisions. Allow God to use the night session, dreams, rest, or lack of sleep to help direct you in your decision making.

4. Train your senses to discern between good and evil. Pay attention to your senses. Do not shut them down during important times in your life.

PROSPERITY PRAYER

We are not alone in life. Holy Spirit, You are always near to help us discern what is good, right, and needed in teaching moments and with each person we encounter. Let us follow You closely and help us to see what the Father is doing in all situations, so that no matter the intention or the hearts of others, we can truly thrive.

CREATING HOLISTIC PROSPERITY

 Relationships and Family: There are dozens of ways to communicate. When we use discernment, we can pick up on unspoken clues about our friends and family to better connect with them.

 Spiritual: When you go into a home, use discernment to know what to say, what not to say, and how to manage your spiritual health in that environment.

 Health: Our bodies are always giving us clues as to what they need. Type 2 diabetes communicates the need to eat a certain way and change behaviors. In the same way, we need to be willing to discern where pain is coming from to address the underlying issue.

Professional: One of the best forms of negotiation is consolidated appraisal from discernment. It helps you to predict something someone might want.

 Mindset: Discern which judgments about yourself are from God and which ones are from your flesh, a reaction to your wounding experiences, or other sources. Only accept judgments that bring life.

 Social: Discernment is one of the best things you can use to vote on leaders and teachers who will help and strengthen your community, as it helps you pick up on nuances and understanding.

26

Loss

For you know the grace of our Lord Jesus Christ,
that though He was rich, yet for your sake He
became poor, so that you through His poverty
might become rich.

—2 CORINTHIANS 8:9

As humans we are guaranteed to experience a few things. Loss is one of them. There is no way we can avoid it. It will happen to us and the people around us in small and big ways. Loss can be accompanied by deep emotions like pain, anger, and sadness. It's very challenging, and everyone responds differently to personal loss. What if there was a way through the pain, through the challenge, through the confusion, to gain something out of our loss or the loss of others?

Well, there is a way—many ways, in fact. Loss is actually positioned from God as a way of prosperity. Unless a seed falls to the ground and dies it can produce no good fruit (John 12:24). Personally, a moment of loss can be repurposed into gain through priceless, life-long experience. We can also be positioned to capitalize on the loss of others for our personal gain in wise, honorable ways.

Repositioning loss financially is no different from doing so in any other area of life. When we are looking for that "deal," often the deal is available because someone else has suffered a loss. If we are patient in our financial decisions, we can pounce on these opportunities to bring a tremendous upside. For example, Warren Buffett, who is arguably one of the greatest investors of all time, uses loss for his financial gain as a primary way to grow his portfolio. In 2008 the world economy was down, and many stocks were affected. Buffett decided to invest and reinvest in bank stocks like Wells Fargo, knowing that they would recover in a few years' time. This has made him a lot of money.

We need to resist the idea that loss determines our outcome in any way. We can train our hearts and minds to not fear loss but instead fear God and align with heaven to imagine and create the best-case scenario for restoration, redemption, or positive impact. Those who recover quickly from loss are those who tell themselves a story with a positive outcome. Those who tell themselves a story where loss is the end, or where loss devastates them, will struggle with more mental, emotional, and psychological challenges.

When we encounter financial loss, we could leverage that loss and write it off on our personal and corporate taxes. Have you ever considered the phantom income of depreciation? In real estate you can strategically capitalize on your depreciating assets almost like receiving another source of income. The tool of loss can be important in our financial planning. Write off losses in a strategic way that will positively benefit you every year.

With Jesus, loss is power for transformation. He was able to leverage His loss in order to gain us. Just as Jesus was able to leverage loss, we should consider doing so as well. Our financial soil is like that of a seed ready for harvesting. The seed may be dead, but once it gets into our hands it will see life again. Paul wrote, "Whatever gain I had, I counted as loss" (Philippians 3:7 ESV).

BUILDING YOUR PROSPEROUS FINANCIAL LIFE

Loss could be your new favorite investment strategy. When you consider spending or investing, first consider what ways you can find a deal. Look for ways to be wise and clever by not always paying a premium for what you are looking for.

- Think of the last time you were able to capitalize on a loss.
- Analyze your personal and corporate financial opportunities. What ways can you assess loss as an investment strategy?
- Explore ways to maximize your profitability when you see the loss of others. Discounts, auctions, short sales, stocks, and so on.

PROSPERITY PRAYER

God, You are our strategic partner. You look into each and every area where we may have loss and help us reposition it to gain just as You have done, Jesus, with millions of decisions You were presented with. Thank You, God, that Your redemption doesn't stop with loss. You can redeem anything and bring it to a better place. Thank You, Lord, for Your plans, insight, and wisdom. We love it. Keep it coming.

CREATING HOLISTIC PROSPERITY

 Relationships and Family: Loss unites relationships. In times of vulnerability we can see the outpouring of support and love from our families and have the privilege to give support to them.

 Spiritual: We are called to lose everything that hinders us from running our race. To lose our life is to gain salvation.

 Health: Being aware of how we are losing or may lose our health or happiness can motivate us to change our behavior before it is too late.

 Professional: Losing a job can be a catalyst for change and for God to open up better opportunities and jobs that we would not otherwise have pursued.

 Mindset: Loss helps us to recognize our value system and reminds us of what is important to us in life. It causes us to think about using our time wisely and reminds us that we can also lose our unhealthy mindsets and be empowered in our thoughts.

 Social: Loss can be painful, but it also grounds us in who we are. When we lose friends or a social group, it allows us to draw close to God, understand who we are, and then enter our next relationships with more strength and steadfastness. Loss can create an opportunity where we can all cover one another's needs and care for one another.

27

Hope in God

Instruct those who are rich in this present world not to be conceited or to fix their hope on the uncertainty of riches, but on God, who richly supplies us with all things to enjoy.
—1 TIMOTHY 6:17

*O*ur hearts follow the invisible path of who and what we place our hope in. If our path of hope is in God, we will be richly supplied with all things. The realization of financial provision in one's life needs to be considered around how capable God is. If He is our ultimate Provider and all provision is in Him, then we can place our faithful expectation of good in God for every area of life.

When we hope in God, we rightly position ourselves to check

in with God and partner with Him. We often do not consider God in financial planning, investments, or purchasing and thus don't put any expectation or hope in Him. However, God wants to show us the depths of His richness and supply us with all His abundance if we hope in Him. My financial provision changes when I place my hope in God. I am open to more options than before.

I (Jeremy) check in with God and ask Him what His hopes and dreams are for the year. Each year I ask God how much income I can walk into. How many streams of income are available to me? What ways can I increase my income and decrease expenditures? After all the goals are set, Ally and I hope in Him. We press into Him. We look for His provision and partner with it.

Our job is our way of connection with His provision for His vision. Hoping in God opens us up to a world of possibilities where finances come into play. God feeds the birds of the air. If He provides for sparrows, how much more so will He provide for you? The question is, Can God provide for us outside of our nine-to-five? Yes! Absolutely.

Let's get practical with God's provision. It requires partnership. He provides for our needs all the time, but God doesn't want us to sit back and rely on Him like entitled children who feel they should be cared for when they do not care for themselves. If we actively engage in hope, we better align with God's provision. We should be constantly asking ourselves what we can do today to walk into these promises. Partner in your finances with hope in God. Hope in God that He will turn things around and get you back on your feet.

To have hope in God is an invitation, and partnering with God in finances is a leveling-up tool. He creates all wealth. He invites you but does not force you to work with Him. One practical way to do this is to ask God how much He wants you to make. You need not put your hope in one man or woman or business or job more than in God. Instead, ask God how to partner with Him in finances in ways you may not even know to think about or expect. When we hope in

God, we do not allow worry about finances to pull us down or drag us in the wrong direction. Hope in God will show us the way to full prosperity.

BUILDING YOUR PROSPEROUS FINANCIAL LIFE

There are so many opportunities for thriving financially as we actively partner our faith with actions. Do your actions with money align with your faith? Do you lean on your own understanding for your finances, or do you spend your finances based on God's plan? Take one action today to show your partnership with God's financial plan for your life.

- Ask God to help you be aware of how much He intends for you to make this year. How might you partner with that?
- Ask God to help you see how much you can save this year. What would you need to do to start saving?
- Ask God to help you see how much you can give this year. What would you need to do to start giving?
- Research how to create and stay on a budget to demonstrate your partnership with and hope in God.

PROSPERITY PRAYER

God, we look to You, where our health comes from. In You we place our expectation and hope. You have the keys to our future. We hope in You with our finances. We hope in You for all of our needs to be covered and our desires to be fulfilled. Thank You for the abundant provision You give to us. We love You, Jesus.

CREATING HOLISTIC PROSPERITY

 Relationships and Family: By hoping in God, you can impact others in your family to hope in God as well and help your family and friends thrive in hard times.

 Spiritual: God is invisible. He has the keys to unlock the invisible things we are seeking and hoping for in our lives. Things like love, joy, peace, and other fruits of the Spirit. The posture of our hearts generates hope for our spiritual connection with Him to bear fruit.

 Health: Instead of just having hope that things will get better, place your hopeful expectations in God to bring about His promises regarding your health. You can have hope that He will help you restore your health and give you a sound mind and peace when your own strength does not bridge the gap between where you are and where you want to be.

 Professional: God is the Author of our faith and our journey. He has an intrigue and desire for our professional walk, and He wants to take us there and help us even more than we want to be helped. We can place our hope in Him to steer and guide us.

 Mindset: Have the mindset that God carries hope for you even when you can't feel or see hope yourself. You are never without Him and never without hope because you can always turn to Him to partner with the hope He has for you.

Social: Hope in God for our nation, just as Israel did. Even on US currency we have the saying "In God We Trust," which reminds us that God is active and involved in bringing prosperity to us as a nation.

28

Thanksgiving

Jesus then took the loaves, gave thanks, and distributed to those who were seated as much as they wanted. He did the same with the fish.
—JOHN 6:11 NIV

Jesus took the bread loaves and the fish, gave thanks, and then fed more than five thousand people. Thankfulness is the bedrock for opportunity. Finances are a provision just like food. In the scripture above, Jesus thanked God, then the provision came forth in ways no mind could comprehend. Thankfulness is not just a feeling; it is a declaration and an action that releases a new reality. It is a principle we need to master to have prosperous lives. In our podcast, *Ways of Prosperity*, we end each episode talking about something big or small that we are thankful for because thankfulness is foundational to prosperity and a healthy mind.

Our ability to recognize what we have been given helps calibrate our hearts around prosperous thinking. It provides a foundation for us to be rightly positioned for our next season or upgrade. Jesus took the little that He had and, with proper alignment, applied it for success. Thanksgiving removes the barriers so that we can properly engage this next season. Mindsets and actions that may be getting in the way of our financial prosperity are removed because thankfulness transforms our minds to be more like the mind of Christ, through whom we can do all things.

One scientific term that could be associated with a transforming mind is *neuroplasticity*, which means that the brain is living and adaptable. It can change its neural pathways and synapses. It can change how we see the world as we learn and experience it. One experience that can change the brain is the discipline of gratitude. People often think of being thankful as something passive that spontaneously happens. But being thankful is an intentional practice of exposing our brains to a new way of thinking, which has the power to literally transform our neural pathways.

There are many ways that thanksgiving can increase our financial status. First, we receive upgrades of being liked and loved and favored for better positions, gifts, promotions, and increase. Second, we can receive an upgrade of provision from heaven, just as Jesus multiplied the fish with thanksgiving, we can supernaturally multiply what we have with thanksgiving. Third, being thankful increases our emotional state, which empowers us to enjoy work, work harder, feel better about saving, and gain more favor with man. Have you noticed that when you feel grateful, you are likely to feel more relaxed and motivated and have more energy and focus, better self-esteem, and more productivity? All this can add to your finances as well.

Sometimes thankfulness has financial benefits we could never even plan for. A while back we were on a cruise. We were sad to notice that most people did not treat the staff well. In fact, most people were downright mean and rude to them. We decided to go out of our way to enthusiastically thank these people for their service. We asked questions about their lives and thoughts and demonstrated our thankfulness in our words and behavior. We talked to their bosses and expressed how we were grateful for the staff and how well they were doing.

We were not expecting to financially prosper because of this. It was one of the furthest things from our minds. But our actions opened up doors, and we were provided exclusive discounts and offers. There were coffee, internet, and food discounts given without solicitation, all because we demonstrated genuine gratitude. This is the power of thankfulness. We can each enter into thankfulness and open up financial doors of opportunity in our current season of life.

BUILDING YOUR PROSPEROUS FINANCIAL LIFE

When we struggle with gratitude, often it is because we have become used to the things we have. Here is an exercise to increase your gratitude today:

1. Look around your home and be intentional to remember or imagine how you felt about your things when you first got them.
2. Consider how you got those things. Be grateful for the people who worked to help you get them.
3. Think about any current bills. Consider how hard life would be without the ability to pay for the services those bills provide. Consider appreciation for shelter, temperature control, lights, water, phones, and so on.

4. Express thankfulness for everyone who has helped you pay for things. Notice how your emotions toward your finances shift when you lead with thankfulness.

PROSPERITY PRAYER

Time and time again You show us how thankfulness opens up doors of possibility. You fed the five thousand and had leftovers because of thankfulness. We want to enter into the abundance of what You have to offer. Help us to tune our hearts and minds toward thankfulness and open up the natural and supernatural doors of opportunity. Thank You, God, for showing us what it means to be thankful. You are the perfect model for this.

CREATING HOLISTIC PROSPERITY

Relationships and Family: Gratitude increases fondness and mutual appreciation. Tell friends and family often how thankful you are for them, and watch your relationships grow in intimacy and joy. Don't wait to tell them you appreciate them.

Spiritual: Gratitude opens the door to spiritual growth and provision. The posture of our hearts toward God should be thankfulness. This helps us to receive more of who He is because we recognize Him. We can always be grateful for what He has done in the past, even if we don't see what He is doing in the present.

Health: Gratitude changes your emotional state, bringing tranquility to your mind and body. It lowers your blood pressure and increases the strength of your immune system.

 Professional: Gratitude opens doors for honesty and mutual appreciation. If you feel unappreciated at work, start offering appreciation to others and see what happens.

 Mindset: Remembering and being thankful for where you have come from and how you have grown keeps you changing, growing, and learning.

 Social: We can be thankful through community ceremonies and actions like tipping those who serve us. We can be thankful together in celebrations. When we celebrate together it helps to establish communities.

PART 5

Increasing Professional Prosperity

With so many hours of your life put toward work, the biggest question is, What are you building at the end of your day, year, and lifetime? How are you serving your community through your occupation? We have the ability to professionally thrive at work through God's guidance and a well-executed plan. *The Ways of Prosperity* gives us that guidance to deploy the right behavior, plan, and response to advance in any project or situation. Our workplace relationships are vital to our success and growth in our field of choice. The cultivation of those relationships is our divine invitation. We also have gifts, skills, and tools to assist us to thrive at work to produce the best outcomes, products, and services. God loves to work. So should we!

29

Dreams

Now Joseph said to Pharaoh, "Pharaoh's dreams are one and the same; God has told to Pharaoh what He is about to do. . . . Behold, seven years of great abundance are coming in all the land of Egypt; and after them seven years of famine will come, and all the abundance will be forgotten in the land of Egypt, and the famine will ravage the land."

—GENESIS 41:25, 29-30

God loves to speak to us at night when we are fast asleep. Ally has heard it said that He speaks to us in the night because we are too preoccupied to listen during the day. A dream is a vision in the night wrapped up in parabolic language. It is God's way to seal instruction in us and place us on a journey to discover the treasure of possibility for our days. Who doesn't love a good romantic chase with clues and love notes around every corner?

Dreams have been a primary way God has chosen to speak since the beginning of time. His voice is everywhere, and therefore dreams can affect every area of our lives. Now, not all dreams are from God. Some dreams can be from our subconscious minds, the by-products of our stresses, thoughts, and desires, our natural and spiritual discernment, and the Devil. However, when we dream at night with God, our plans are perfected and our ways are established.

It is beautiful to see dreams transcend into our professional walk, occupations, hobbies, and work life. Yes! God is keenly interested in what jobs we have and how successful we are at work. So much so that He would speak to us at night to assist our sometimes hectic workdays. He wants to give us His creative advantage so we are rightly positioned for our best life.

Joseph was a dreamer and a dream interpreter (Genesis 41). God gave Joseph the interpretation of his boss's dream to save the company of people he was leading. Joseph was an integral part in the survival of everyone who lived in Egypt. He deployed systems and measures for people to plan in the years of abundance and famine.

I (Ally) have had the privilege in therapy to connect with people about their dreams. People come into sessions and divulge their spiritual journeys and process what happens in their dream lives. I work to help them understand the imagery, symbolism, their feelings, and associated thoughts that surround their dreams. I get excited about the opportunities to help them interpret (spiritually and scientifically) their own dreams. I feel positioned like Joseph to bring about the best interpretation of the sealed instruction for their lives and occupations at work. Working with dreams enhances my relationships with clients, my work, and the feedback I receive from clients. I have found that most people feel their dreams have some meaning behind them.

Dreams are God's version of drip content for us to forever stay plugged into His narrative. The key to unlocking the mysterious, cryptic, and sometimes over-the-top symbolism is for us to understand our own process. We need to make up our mind on what we think and believe about certain things. Are lions a symbol of power and love or are they scary? After the dream consider what perspective it was in. What was your proximity to the main theme? Your role? Your feelings? What message are you getting? God will use any and all of it to speak to you.

Professionally, dreams have been a catalyst in my (Jeremy's) life for more than fifteen years. I was previously employed at a company when God gave me a vivid dream of an aircraft carrier going down. I was able to safely jump and land into my next vehicle. The other employees in the dream were not able to make it out so smoothly, and they were going to lose years of their life stuck on the crashed plane. I knew the company I worked for was going to implode, and it was time to start looking for the next opportunity. During my next trip, I was on an elevator and heard God say, "I have a job for you." Upon first introduction, the next couple I met offered me a job that led me into a beautiful new season of life. The first company dissolved in twelve months, and the new job became the most seamless transition and upgrade I could have imagined.

BUILDING YOUR PROSPEROUS PROFESSIONAL LIFE

We can prosper by showing an interest in others, and sometimes this means helping them understand themselves. Dreams are a great way to do this. Most people dream, and most people believe there is some meaning in their dreams.

1. Simply asking your family, coworkers, and friends about their interesting or strange dreams can open up a sacred conversation. They will feel you are interested in them and care about them. You don't even have to bring up God, but you can.
2. Once someone tells you about a dream, ask about items, places, and people in the dream. Ask what those might mean symbolically and how that might relate to their present life.
3. Without even interpreting the dream, you might gain insight, and they will gain the feeling that you care about the things they care about. They will likely trust and appreciate you more for it.

PROSPERITY PRAYER

Jesus, You are the keeper of the night season. Protect our minds and hearts at night so we only hear from You. Go before us and seal up the wonderful instruction of the Father into our daily lives. We long to know the secrets of Your heart that You desire to share with us. Whisper sweet things to us in our night seasons so we may love You more. We bless You, Jesus, for speaking to us in our dreams. May our dreams grow our connection with You and impact the world that Your heart loves.

CREATING HOLISTIC PROSPERITY

 Relationships and Family: Dreams give insight about your connections and where you can speak the heart of God into their lives. God shares secrets so you can relate to them, understand them, and get to know God's heart for them.

 Spiritual: Dreams help you to pursue God for understanding. They are the language of heaven that allow us to have an ongoing conversation with God. Even when our minds are full, He can seal instruction in the night.

 Health: Dreams create opportunities for emotional stability as God reveals His thoughts about the future and gives you the best-case scenario you can work toward. This helps you set goals.

 Financial: Dreams give you understanding of when provision is coming, when to transition jobs, when to save for times of famine, and so on. God speaks in dreams and cares deeply about your financial stability.

 Mindset: Dreams establish the fact that God can speak to us any time He wants. Dreams from God help to forever shape our mindsets.

 Social: Dreams can promote community and social connection. God gives us dreams to influence our communities.

30

Favor with Man

*[They were] praising God and having favor with
all the people. And the Lord was adding to their
number day by day those who were being saved.*

—ACTS 2:47

The idea of favor is not a new one. Most commonly, favor is used to communicate a request for assistance. We are not referring to this kind of favor today. There are two categories of favor that are discussed in this book: the favor of God and the favor of man. Let's explore the favor of man. It is the natural and spiritual preference shown to someone in the giving of one's influence, abilities, resources, and open doors. It is the mutual giving of someone's access, an upgrade from the status quo.

Everywhere people are, the possibility of favor exists. Have you ever befriended someone and they upgraded a part of your life by simply inviting you into theirs? That is the favor of man at its finest. We can also see the realization of favor in our workplace. Doors of possibility for promotions and raises can open without any effort on your behalf. When you have favor with man, people are attracted to you like a magnet. Your value and appreciation increase, and people recognize your giftings and strengths. You may be given the next opportunity above others simply because of the favor.

At the outset, opportunities that seem impossible begin to open up. New contracts are mutually given with more favorable terms for you, and vendors may provide services for a lower cost without negotiation. Favor at work increases profitability and productivity. I (Ally) experienced an example of favor with man several years ago. My mentor at the time encouraged me to attend conferences with the goal of increasing my professional network. So I traveled out of town for an upcoming conference.

When I arrived, I noticed an older man sitting by himself with no one to talk to. I struck up a conversation with him about one of the talks we had just listened to. He then asked what I did. I shared that I had to quit a job at a psychology-based treatment center because the required hours would not work around my doctoral training schedule. I expressed my wish to keep working through my training because I liked to work and help others.

The man told me he was the CEO of a large chain of treatment centers and wanted to give me a job that would fit around my schedule. It was a job I ended up loving and learning from more than any other I'd ever had. This is favor with man. I did nothing supernatural or extraordinary but was extended favor for my new job.

I thought about being brought before the kings and queens of our day and having favor with them just as the Bible says. Esther, Ruth, David, and Joseph in the Bible are other examples of people who had favor with man and prospered because of it. Their position, income, and influence were changed. They were elevated to a new place God had for them. They were not always the most qualified, but it never happened without their partnership and effort. As we grow in our relationships, connections, and emotional intelligence, we can increase in our favor with man. We can make giant strides in our professional journeys with one moment of favor!

BUILDING YOUR PROSPEROUS PROFESSIONAL LIFE

Part of how we gain favor is simply through the law of sowing and reaping. The more favor you give, the more you will start to receive. Here are a few questions to help you assess how you're engaging in this principle:

- What is a way you would like to be favored in work? Is it through a raise, promotion, opportunity, or new job? With connections? Or with something else?
- Identify ways you can favor those you work with and identify things that might help them feel favored.
- On a scale of one to one hundred, how much favor do you think you're giving to your boss, your clients, and your customers? Start with a realistic number and consider how you might increase that number today.

PROSPERITY PRAYER

God, You are the God of possibility. It is incredible to see You soften the hearts of men and women to bring them into a new season of influence and favor. God, we ask You to pull back the veil over our hearts and minds from those we should bestow favor upon. Teach us Your ways. Guide us into divine favor everywhere we go. Thank You, Jesus, for Your favor. Help us to be good stewards of all that You give us.

CREATING HOLISTIC PROSPERITY

 Relationships and Family: As you care about others, you increase favor in relationships. It is as if an invisible barrier is open and the people around you can see your potential. They want to be with you, work with you, and spend time with you.

 Spiritual: God can lead you into the most favorable relationships, if you let Him. As you experience the favor of man and give favor, you can have a greater understanding and awareness of how the favor of God is displayed.

 Health: When you have favor with man, people will be happy to work harder to make you happy and help you heal in mind and body.

 Financial: You get the best options. When you need the expert, you can find an expert who can work with your price. When you need a good employee, you find one. Your connections become financial sources of prosperity when you ask yourself, Who do I know? What do we need that we can give one another?

Mindset: Valuing yourself enables others to see you with favor and value you as well.

 Social: Pursuing favor with man opens up relational doors, connections, and opportunities to share God's love in your community. Favor allows others to see you accurately for who you really are.

31

Kindness

But the LORD was with Joseph and extended kindness to him, and gave him favor in the sight of the chief jailer. The chief jailer committed to Joseph's charge all the prisoners who were in the jail; so that whatever was done there, he was responsible for it. The chief jailer did not supervise anything under Joseph's charge because the LORD was with him; and whatever he did, the LORD made to prosper.

—GENESIS 39:21–23

K indness is a corporate currency at work and in the exchange of a product or service. Businesses thrive when they throw in a little extra kindness in the way they treat customers or clients. Most people and companies don't realize that we are all in the business of serving others regardless of what product or service is being sold. Companies can launch a new product and have great success for a season. But one day someone is going to come along with a similar product, and they will deploy kindness along with it. The second company will win every time.

The Lord introduced us to kindness by extending it to Joseph. This brought an extension of care and prosperity. Whatever he did, the Lord made to prosper! Wow. What an incredible thing that can happen with kindness. Joseph was looked after, protected, and blessed with God's blessing and favor. He was brought up under the wings of God and cared for in ways that only God could provide. This is the extension of kindness.

For companies, owners, and bosses, treating your employees well increases their commitment to the company. Employees are more invested when their bosses are interested in who they are. Gary Vaynerchuk, a serial entrepreneur, wrote a book about kindness in the workplace. He talks about getting to know his employees. He asks them questions to dive into their process: "What are your honest goals here? I want to help you achieve them." "Tell me what motivates you in life because I want to support that." "Do you love to hike or go bike riding?" "Do you want to take all my employees and start a new firm? I support you and care about you. I will be the first person to invest in your company." His kindness and judgment-free mindsets are truly amazing.

Being genuine, sincere, and kind is the greatest possible customer service. Imagine a boss was thinking of two candidates for a job. They appeared to be equal in most ways, but one was kind and one was not. The kind applicant would get the job. In graduate school, I (Ally) was given instruction on how to interview, and one of the big tips was to be kind and supportive of other interviewees. Many people know to be kind to the secretary and the people who currently work there, but it sets someone apart when they are in competition with someone for a position and they are kind and supportive of them.

The kindness of others is another way we may be led into prosperity. One of our friends went through a season when he was not making much money at all. He was, however, following what God called him to do and working hard with all his heart. God provided for him through the kindness of others. This allowed him to focus on growing in his professional skills without the stress of money. God led a family to him who offered to let him stay in their home, eat their food, and not have to pay rent. Their kindness made a way for him to prosper and grow professionally in the direction God called him. God provides in far more ways than money.

I (Ally) believe kindness is a key to a successful work environment, both with superiors and clients and with those in lower positions. I try to take the time to find out how to support the person, not just their role. I do not expect their humanity to go away just because they are in charge. We all want to feel seen, understood, and supported—even our bosses! If they are often stressed, find ways to help them de-stress. If they are angry, our not reacting with anger helps as well. If they are accusatory, we can try to understand what they see, and why, to help them reach a collaborative place where they feel safe and reassured. Often this leads to favor and promotion in the workplace. Kindness changes everything.

BUILDING YOUR PROSPEROUS PROFESSIONAL LIFE

Leaders are far more judged than others because there are often many expectations placed on them, and some may be unrealistic. Build a prosperous life today by showing kindness to one person above or more advanced than you, and one person below or less advanced. Here are some ideas to start with:

- Call them up just to say thank you for whatever good they have done and encourage them.
- Write a card of appreciation.
- Send a small gift.
- Look for a way to reduce their frustration and make their work life easier.

PROSPERITY PRAYER

Thank You, Jesus, for being so kind to us. We love You and love everything You bring. Your kindness brings nations to Your love. Thank You for extending Your kindness to us. We will cherish every extension of Your love. The world experienced kindness first in You, Jesus, and we will forever follow You in our homes, workplaces, and lives. We love You, Jesus.

CREATING HOLISTIC PROSPERITY

Relationships and Family: Acts of kindness are a way to empower connection. Strategically employ acts of kindness to build your relationships. Planning them ahead of time does not decrease their impact.

Spiritual: As a Christian, you have access to the unlimited kindness of the Father. Receive as much as you can of His kindness. Notice it, dwell on it, tapping into God's heart for a person, place, or thing.

Health: Be kind to yourself. If you are not kind to yourself, you will not be in a place of peace. If you are not in a place of peace, you are more likely to be unkind to others. You are worthy of God's kindness, and rejecting the kindness of God is rejecting Him.

 Financial: If you are kind to people, you will get better deals and financial terms in negotiation.

 Mindset: Aim to think ten kind thoughts for each negative or self-critical thought you think about yourself.

 Social: Extend God's kindness to people that others might not accept or value. We imitate Christ in this way, and we demonstrate His nature and the way He extended kindness to us when we were unacceptable to God and unworthy.

32

Friendships

Two are better than one because they have a good return for their labor. For if either of them falls, the one will lift up his companion. But woe to the one who falls when there is not another to lift him up.

—ECCLESIASTES 4:9–10

Good friendships are powerful! We can do so much more when we are with friends who work with us, believe in us, and support us. Ecclesiastes says it best: "Two are better than one." We would like to believe that most of us already live by this scripture in our personal lives. We love our friends and know that things are way better when they are around. Have we yet considered what it would be like to pursue genuine friendships at work? Such as being friends with your boss?

Consider God's promise in the workplace. He positions us with friends at work so we can be more productive, creative, and supportive. He knows what we need. Maybe the thing missing in your work is the right friend to help you find solutions. Friendship at work can provide many benefits: having a better work environment, creating connections, getting new opportunities, accessing a support network, increasing labor, and so on. Thinking about having friends at work will help you elevate your accomplishments and happiness overall if they are not compartmentalized. Some swear off having friends at work, thinking that work is not about making friends. However, work is not meant to be about isolation either.

All good friendships show us more about who God is and how loved and known we are by Him. Companionship is a key to our prosperity. The biblical basis for friendship at our workplace is strong. For example, Jesus could have gone about the Father's business on His own instead of including the disciples. The disciples were also told to go out two by two when they worked to further the kingdom. Paul called Priscilla and Aquila his coworkers (Romans 16:3). Joseph was rescued because he made a friend in prison who provided a professional connection to Pharaoh, who needed Joseph's dream-interpretation skills.

Friendships also create security that empowers us toward success. They can act as iron to sharpen us as well as provide strengths that complement ours. They can provide support, encouragement, accountability, and a sounding board. There is a reason some of the top organizations hold think tanks. Instead of one perspective, they receive multiple perspectives.

I (Ally) found friends to be vital when I started a new job: asking for help, sharing ideas, or helping one another remember codes or certain procedures for documenting encounters. Friends are safe people you can grow and learn with. You can ask them for help and be vulnerable without fear of judgment. They help you perform better at work, help you think in new ways, and make things easier as they provide their knowledge, insight, support, and perspective when you feel stuck.

This way of prosperity is evident in so many areas. God wants us to thrive in our workplaces, and He knows this is only possible with strong, supportive friends. We can be friends with the people we work with. Open your heart to the possibility of becoming friends with your supervisor and boss, remembering to maintain appropriate respect for their positions. If they are on your team, your productivity and prosperity will increase in ways superior to that of your peers who are not in those relationships. Friends are truly from God.

BUILDING YOUR PROSPEROUS PROFESSIONAL LIFE

Be intentional to nurture a friendship today. Mirroring is one tool that causes another person to feel known, to be more relaxed, and to lower their defenses. Mirroring can be a powerful tool to help others feel connected to you in the workplace. Here is how to mirror:

1. Enter conversations with the intention of listening to the other person's words and observing that person's body language.
2. After the person says something, do one of two things. Either repeat a few of their key words as a question back to them, in a curious tone, or summarize what they said in a few words.
3. The person will tend to respond by opening up more about who they are, what they value, the hard parts about their job, or what they want in life.
4. This sense of connectedness helps you get to know them in a deeper way and begin to develop a friendship that can benefit

you both. The next time you need help, this person will be more likely to want to help you.

Example: Mirroring can be as simple as someone at work saying, "The project is going well, but I am looking forward to vacation." Then you say, curiously, "You're looking forward to vacation?" See how they respond with more information about themselves and their thoughts.

PROSPERITY PRAYER

You are my best Friend, and You contribute to the prosperity of others every day by helping us when we fall, guiding us, and providing us with companionship. Teach us to be the kind of friend that You are to the world. Jesus, You have been our best Friend in every time of need. Help us build the best relationships at home, work, and other places.

CREATING HOLISTIC PROSPERITY

 Relationships and Family: Mutually connected friendship circles can bring positive introductions and relationships. A family member's friend group may contain your new best friend.

 Spiritual: Iron sharpens iron (Proverbs 27:17), and friendships help us grow spiritually.

Health: Friends can motivate us to be healthy: friends can work out with us, cook with us, and realign our emotions toward health.

 Financial: Friends can provide financial connections and accountability to spend wisely.

 Mindset: Two are better than one (Ecclesiastes 4:9). Whatever challenge or mindset you may have, you are more likely to have a great victory when you have help.

 Social: Good friends in our community will shoulder our burdens with us so we can make it through tough times. They can also encourage us toward a common goal.

33

Honor

Honor the LORD from your wealth
And from the first of all your produce;
So your barns will be filled with plenty
And your vats will overflow with new wine.
—PROVERBS 3:9-10

We can grow in our companies above our peers. We can have the best relationships and be liked by most people. We can excel in our connections and get the best deals. All this is possible when we lift up our peers, coworkers, and bosses in high esteem. This positions us for the best professional and relational exchange. If we desire to grow in our companies, we should build a foundation of honor. Honor brings abundance because the person giving honor is rightly positioned to serve best, regardless of class, rank, or title.

Honor is servant-minded. It provides recognition, access, and kindness to the person or company being honored. Over the years, I (Jeremy) have spent a lot of time with people who honor well. I have watched them honor when they could easily have been dishonoring. For example, a friend refuses to speak negative things about someone unless he is speaking to the person directly. He guards his tongue to make sure only wholesome words are exchanged with their peers about that person. Also, another friend might disagree with someone 99 percent of the time, but they will only confess to their friends about the 1 percent they agree with in order to hold up a standard of being loving.

Showing honor can open doors because it communicates that you are a safe person who will protect the interests of others and not put them down for being vulnerable. It is a relational connection and a way of truly seeing others through God's eyes. We often think of honor as something we do for someone important, successful, or good. However, honor should be given to those around us not because of who they are but because of who God says they are.

Honor through kindness and servanthood in a professional environment might seem counterproductive, but it is the model to success and prosperity that Jesus showed us. This is true with our coworkers, customers, and clients. I (Ally) once worked with someone who told a story about how they had honored a client. The client was going through a hard time. Others had spoken to the client her whole life about who she wasn't, what was wrong with her, and what she needed to change.

The person was adversarial, and others did not feel happy or safe around her. Instead of commenting on that, my coworker commented on the client's strengths and positive qualities. The woman started crying for the first time, and her behavior changed drastically as she had a vision for what God saw for her life and it resonated with her. Honor changed the situation, and this approach did not go unnoticed by my friend's boss. This was one of the things that later led to a promotion.

If we make it our goal to treat employees so well that they do not want to leave, we prosper more. Honoring bosses ask their employees, "How can I help you meet your goals? What do you need?" If we treat our bosses well, they want to continue to work with us and promote us. Honored employees grab hold of their bosses' vision and work for them just as they would be working for God. This is how we thrive. I often ask myself, "How can I make my supervisor feel like they are doing well? How can I calm their nerves? How can I support them? What do they need to feel safe and known?" Honor releases life! We can all professionally prosper when we fill our hearts and minds with honor toward those around us. We will experience so much blessing that it will overtake us.

BUILDING YOUR PROSPEROUS PROFESSIONAL LIFE

One way of honoring others is by overlooking and covering mistakes with grace. This is not a long-term solution to everything, but often when you start to dishonor others in your heart, your behavior follows and you become unhappy at your work. Your behavior then becomes an obstacle to your advancement in the company or relationship. By using the following process, you create honor for them and a better workplace for yourself. Here are a few steps to take:

1. Take deep breaths to allow your logical thinking to come back online and replace or supplement your emotional thinking.

2. Suspend your judgment and any destructive or hurtful comments to create a feeling of safety between the two of you.

3. See these situations as an opportunity to brainstorm creative solutions together and help one another get out of a bind.

4. Expect you will find a good outcome and you will be more likely to find it.

5. Continue intentionally sowing seeds of honor that you can hope to reap when you make a mistake, are misunderstood, or have a problem.

PROSPERITY PRAYER

Jesus, You are the best at honoring. You only speak love and kindness to us and cover us. Thank You for coming in to serve even when we rejected You. Honor opened up our hearts. We pray that we can be like You and honor those around us. Thank You for this way of prosperity. Train us to be as honoring as You are.

CREATING HOLISTIC PROSPERITY

Relationships and Family: Look for something to praise and celebrate about those closest to you. This increases your prosperity as they will trust you more, feel seen by you, and be happy to grow closer to you.

Spiritual: The recognition and exchange of any reward one receives is giving it back to Jesus. This is the best way to honor God. It increases the potential for a healthy relationship with Him and puts us in proper alignment with what He is doing in us so we can partner with it.

Health: Honor your body, the temple of God. Be thankful and appreciate it even if you are not perfectly happy with it. Valuing yourself is part of how you value God. You are more powerful to represent God when you strengthen your emotional and physical health.

 Financial: You can exhibit honor by how you spend what you receive. Every dollar we spend is an extension of who we are. We can spend it in honoring ways or in dishonoring ways that create obstacles for us.

 Mindset: God sets the context for honor; it is up to us to align our thoughts with His. We are encouraged to seek honor (Romans 2:7). We can do this by being diligent to think and act in honorable ways.

 Social: First Peter 2:17 reminds us to honor everyone we come in contact with, including those in authority over where we live. This helps us to prosper by not using our words destructively or making things worse in our community.

34

Considering Options

She considers a field and buys it;
From her earnings she plants a vineyard.
—**PROVERBS 31:16**

A t our place of profession, we should surround ourselves with a multitude of options. It's silly to just consider one way of doing things and be so set on that way working out. We should not simply apply for work at the first place we see without drawing comparisons and conducting more than one interview. The ability to measure good options is in having them. The more options, the better the data will be to make the best choice.

God has always given us options. Starting in the garden of Eden, He has provided us with choices, and the invitation to choose an option is to know that there is not just one right way. This may hurt our pride, but it is better to not be left stranded at the end of a bad option. There is always another choice. Having both plan A and plan B means we are properly using the ways of prosperity. The first idea does not have to be right. Let it go and have a plan B that alleviates the pressure and allows you to improvise if someone or something falls through. You can mediate work problems if you always see options.

A person who uses this often at work will be set apart from their peers. Often, companies, churches, and organizations are slow movers, and they are set on one way of doing things. Having options is better because it creates versatility. Consider multiple options as did the creators of the Waze app. When one road gets congested, there is almost always another option. This app shows us where that other road is. When there is an accident ahead, the Waze app shows a way around the route we thought was the right way. Before traffic apps we would simply waste time behind an accident not knowing what to do.

I (Ally) spent a while considering options for my career and tried several directions before finding a place that I felt matched my calling and gifts. My initial paths were great. I worked as a fitness trainer in my teens, because I loved seeing people's lives transformed. I studied English because I loved complex, metaphorical thinking, reading, and I loved communicating through writing. But those were not the best long-term fit. Finally, I realized the perfect option for me was psychology. It challenged my brain and focused on a transformative process that I loved having in my work. It also allowed me to help people and provide important tools and motivation. I believe I only got there by constantly considering options. I took the time to truly consider what I was good at, how God made me, and what would be satisfying long term. I was not afraid to consider options other than what I was doing at the moment, and now I have been in the field of psychology for almost ten years.

When considering options, the big decisions are not the main focus; in the middle of each day the mundane is pivotal. Which vendor should you choose? Do you have a backup vendor if the contract is delayed? How many contracts should you compare for a venue before having the best bedrock for a decision? Also, how many interviews should you have before you can feel good about the right new hire? These are all questions we should answer in our professional walk. Options create flexibility and the power to always have an alternative.

In the evaluation of options, try to refrain from getting emotionally charged about one until the facts can come through. People tend to react to what feels good versus what is good. When we look at our options at work, we are putting more faith in our abilities and in God's ability to come through for us. It keeps our mind open and creative for new solutions. When we are creative, we can thrive.

BUILDING YOUR PROSPEROUS PROFESSIONAL LIFE

Take a moment and consider the options you have with your current skills.

- Is there a way to multiply your efforts or start a side business?
- Do you have unused skills and interests that might benefit the lives of others?
- Are there skills or services you can offer for free to others with the goal of helping to build your professional network?

PROSPERITY PRAYER

Lord, in all ways You are the best decision maker. You considered us in Your heart and chose us. We considered You and chose You in response. We love how You give us a multitude of options in every area of life, and we delight in finding the best one. Give us Your wisdom to choose rightly and give us Your flexibility to look for more options when needed. Thank You, Jesus.

CREATING HOLISTIC PROSPERITY

Relationships and Family: Avoid having a set way of doing things. Be the person who introduces new, more effective options in your family for relating, celebrating, and doing activities. Be open to multiple options and not just an option that works for you but one that works for others.

Spiritual: One of the best ways to grow or get an upgrade in our spiritual journeys or connection with God is through being tested in our options. In the garden we were presented with different options. Choose the options that do not reject your relationship with God.

Health: Not every therapist and doctor is a good fit for you. It is important to consider different personalities, perspectives, and options for treatment. Not all health professionals are trained the same, have the same interest in their work, or have the same expertise or specialties.

Financial: Consider options when it comes to taxes. Look for ways to reduce your taxes through strategy and wisdom. Consider options to reduce your spending with other insurance providers or stores.

Mindset: Create new options that bridge a gap of frustration. When in a frustrating moment, look at brainstorming or creating a "third option" for each situation.

 Social: Consider options for your community to make it a better or happier place. What are initiatives you can start or join to meet a need to make your community better?

35

Impartation

For I long to see you so that I may impart some
spiritual gift to you, that you may be established.
—ROMANS 1:11

Ne of the easiest ways to get ahead in our professional walk is to glean and receive from others. This is the practical and spiritual process of impartation. Professional impartation is not just for prophets! We see professional impartation across all disciplines. I (Ally) have had several mentors impart to me in the field of psychology. Impartation can come in many forms, including books, words, and modeling of successful habits.

Some of the most popular singers started as backup singers, such as Mariah Carey and John Legend. No doubt they received an impartation of knowledge as backup singers that helped shape them into the performers they became. The same goes for people in almost any field, including hairstylists, law enforcers, pastors, and chefs.

We recently visited a restaurant run by chef Jordan Kahn. While eating, we were reminded of other places we had eaten that were run by the most decorated American chef, Thomas Keller. When the meal was over, we googled Chef Kahn's background and discovered that he studied one of Keller's cookbooks early on, which shaped his love for cooking. He wrote to Keller and before the age of eighteen began an unpaid apprenticeship at one of Keller's restaurants. This is a good example of professional impartation. We could see the connections in the kinds of items on the menu and Kahn's sensibility toward food, even though the presentation of the food could not have been more unique and different.

The apostle Paul urged the Corinthians to follow his example as he followed the example of Christ (1 Corinthians 11:1). This is a way of impartation. It is a model we can follow to improve ourselves and our skills. Impartation opens and invites us into a new season of being established in a gift, ability, or knowledge. It can come from many different people, not just one. "Take My yoke upon you and learn from Me. . . . For My yoke is easy," Jesus proclaimed (Matthew 11:29–30).

I (Jeremy) was blessed to spend a year of my life with Tom and Kathy Miller. Tom worked very hard and became the CIO (chief information officer) of two Fortune 100 companies on two separate occasions. Every day Tom would come home and talk about his workday and what processes were in place to overcome the challenges. Some of these systems were created by Tom, and some were developed by corporate leadership. As you can imagine, they were some of the best in the world. I often think back on this as a remarkable time in my life during which I learned so much.

I was able to take my impartation from Tom's example and carry it into so many areas of my life, including the multiple companies I run. I am now upgraded in life because of that impartation. We can all experience this. Who around us can we grow from? Follow them until you become like them, just as the apostle Paul said. God loves impartation—it was His idea in the first place.

BUILDING YOUR PROSPEROUS PROFESSIONAL LIFE

What professional goals or skills would you like to grow in? Who would you like to receive professional input from? Don't worry about practicality at first—reach for the sky! In your wildest dreams, who would mentor or teach you through example? Now ask yourself a few things:

1. Can you watch videos online of these people offering training or read their books? These are several ways to receive impartation.
2. As you continue to get to know that person (even from a distance), you learn their style and their professional skills. You can then start to ask, What would they do in this situation?
3. Is there is a person in your life or someone that a friend or family member knows who is doing what you would like to be doing?
4. If possible, it is helpful to invite them out to coffee or over for a meal and ask for their wisdom and stories. I (Jeremy) received incredible impartation from a leader by offering to serve him. This is one of the best ways to let the skills and wisdom of others be imparted: helping them and getting to see how they act, think, and respond by being around them.

PROSPERITY PRAYER

Jesus, we look to You to impart to us every spiritual blessing in heavenly places. We love Your impartation. We look to You to pour into the people who are around us so we may receive impartation from them. Thank You for this wonderful tool that we can grow substantially from. We receive what You are doing in us. Thank You, Jesus.

CREATING HOLISTIC PROSPERITY

 Relationships and Family: Family members can impart to one another by modeling ways to solve problems. Families can also impart wisdom about what to do and not do.

 Spiritual: The transfer of spiritual gifts can happen through the laying on of hands, prayer, and words. We can be established in the ways of breakthrough and possibility that the other person carries within them.

 Health: We can be successful in our health as we look to others who can impart the way they achieved their goals for a healthy body.

 Financial: We can receive financial impartation through the legacy of being a wise spender and through receiving an inheritance or money from our families.

Mindset: Look for what the situations in your life may impart: wisdom, experience, or ideas. Have a mindset that everyone can impart something good to you if you take the time to ask about it and that the situations in your life can do the same.

 Social: Through connection and gathering, we can impart to one another and fill the gaps for what we need in our lives. There is corporate impartation for churches and communities where everyone can receive an upgrade together.

PART 6

Increasing Mindsets That Create Prosperity

Thoughts in motion create realities. When we build our cornerstone mindsets around the healthy thought patterns that invite God in, we build a world of endless possibilities. The mind of Christ is creative, brilliant, and empowered. We have been offered the mind of Christ, but have we embraced it? His mind is full of deep, resilient faith and hope but equally full of very practical wisdom. Our thoughts and mindsets are important. Proverbs 23:7 tells us that as a man thinks in his heart, so is he. Scripture teaches us that our thoughts are the triggers that create an outcome of actions and emotions. Are they producing fruitful or unfruitful actions and emotions? Prosperous mindsets produce the optimal fruit and prune away the mindsets that lead us toward unhealthy or unhelpful actions and emotions. This leads us toward the heart of God.

36

Joy

His master said to him, "Well done, good and
faithful servant. You have been faithful and
trustworthy over a little, I will put you in charge
of many things; share in the joy of your master."
—MATTHEW 25:21 AMP

We are a tapestry of hundreds of mindsets formed from experience, education, revelation, and observation. They are the
guardrails of our mental road maps. To start, let's explore the mindset
of joy. You might say, "Joy is a mindset? I thought it was an emotion."
Yes, joy is a mindset and an emotion.

Jesus presents us with a very interesting proposition on joy.
He spoke of joy being much more than a temporary feeling or

satisfaction. He looked at the joy that was set before Him when He endured the cross (Hebrews 12:2). You know who was set before Him that brought Him so much joy? It was you and me! Another time He spoke a parable and said, "Well done, good and faithful servant. You have been faithful over a little; I will set you over much. Enter into the joy of your master" (Matthew 25:23 ESV).

This entrance to joy with the master is far more than an emotion or moment of celebration. It is a perpetual experience of joy. We can experience joy (Jesus) any day of the week. It is a mindset that we can tap into without limitation. If joy is something beyond just our momentary feeling and we are somehow pulled into the Father's delight, then we can ever remain in a joy-filled state despite enduring various trials.

A few years ago, I (Ally) was studying in England. I awoke one night to yelling, drunk students. I soon realized they were stealing my bike outside my window. They cut the lock and took off. Initially, I felt angry because my rights were violated, but as I thought about calling the police or student security, I changed my mindset. I wondered how the bike might bless the students and thought about praying for them. I felt an overwhelming joy by providing a big blessing to someone's life, even if they stole the blessing. I thought about how Jacob stole a blessing and God still blessed him. I internally released the bike to them and asked the Holy Spirit to go with them and rest on the bike and on their hearts so that somehow their experience would lead them to encounter God.

The next day my friends saw the bike was gone and the broken bike lock still on the ground. I told them about my mindset of joy and hope based on my relationship with God. I said all I had belonged to God anyway, so there was no need to waste time being angry or upset. Instead, I would see it as an opportunity or "test" for how to grow in joy that surpasses understanding.

My friends could not understand my response, but they said they were amazed by my joy and faith. They said they had never seen a person react that way or have that mindset when something was stolen, and it made them think twice about how they would react to things in the future. James 1:2–4 says to "consider it pure joy, my brothers and sisters, whenever you face trials of many kinds, because you know that the testing of your faith produces perseverance. Let perseverance finish its work so that you may be mature and complete, not lacking anything" (NIV).

All things can put us on a growth journey so we can enter into our best life. When we count it all joy, we are not excluding the difficult parts of our life. We enter into an eternal state of happiness. God instructs us to have joy because He knows it is the medicine to help us get through. Joy is about being an overcomer. It is found in meaning, not in circumstance. Look ahead because joy is set before you.

BUILDING YOUR PROSPEROUS MINDSET LIFE

Abundant joy doesn't happen randomly, and it doesn't happen overnight. It is something that grows with practice. Focus on increasing joy by 1 percent today and invest in joy that surpasses moods and understanding. Here are some ways to do that:

- Write a list of your five most meaningful things, including people and places. These are the joys that will give you strength and options to focus on in hard times and focus on to create more happy moments.
- Focus on the good things you have. Look around where you live and give three to five minutes of undivided attention to looking at each thing. Think about where it came from, how it got to you, and what you appreciate about it.

- Spend time in nature. Science has proven that nature tends to make us happy. Observe things closely; observe the sounds, smells, textures, and sights.
- Rehearse and relive your happiest memories through looking at pictures or reminiscing with family or friends.
- Watch funny videos and videos in which people are laughing. This triggers your mirror neurons and will automatically help you feel a bit of what they were feeling, which can boost your mood.

PROSPERITY PRAYER

You saw us, Jesus, when You endured the cross. We were Your joy and delight. Thank You, Jesus, for Your continued faith in and love for us. Show us Your eternal state of joy that You delight in from the Father. We desire to enter into the joy of our Master in every situation, big and small. Help us to keep our eyes on You. Thank You for being so joyful all the time. We bless You, Jesus.

CREATING HOLISTIC PROSPERITY

 Relationships and Family: Joy increases bonding and connection, loyalty, and family connectedness.

 Spiritual: Joy strengthens our spirits to help us relate to Jesus. It helps us overcome spiritual challenges and live in spiritual peace and hope.

 Health: Having joy impacts our physical health by reducing stress and cortisol levels.

Financial: Joyfully accept the provision God has provided without comparing it to others. Joy is attractive and it sells! People want joy and are willing to pay for it.

 Professional: Joy gives strength that melts dissension and bitterness, that allows us to maintain creative problem solving and connection with coworkers.

 Social: Joy unites communities, helps us bond, and creates common goals and experiences to work toward.

37

Compassion

Yet the LORD longs to be gracious to you;
therefore he will rise up to show you
compassion.
For the LORD is a God of justice.
Blessed are all who wait for him!
—ISAIAH 30:18 NIV

Mindsets mold and shape us more than the combination of all our stray thoughts. We are a living reflection of those mindsets. Jesus' life is a tremendous source for great mindsets and a renewed mind. Often we turn to Jesus to upgrade our old mindsets and generate new ones. He is a living well that never runs dry. In Him we can find the words and thoughts of life. At every opportunity, Jesus brought people out of the old way of thinking into a new way. He loved to do this by having people experience His compassion.

The mind of Christ is filled with compassion. When Jesus had compassion it led to healing, to feeding the hungry, to spiritual upgrades. It led to provision of all kinds. He also demonstrated the self-compassion He wants us to imitate. In the Garden of Gethsemane He expressed His sorrowful feelings. He expressed His desire not to die, His desire for another solution, and His acceptance of the will of God. He talked with the Father and sought comfort and strength to persevere in a situation He did not like.

Self-compassion is not about letting ourselves off the hook or avoiding hard things. It is about recognizing the truth of a situation and using a tone of kindness and hope toward ourselves and our situations. It is not saying we never do anything wrong. It is being gentle, kind, and forgiving when we do. It is humbly accepting the transformative, healing compassion of Jesus.

Self-compassion leaves the door open to discuss solutions. It is inviting a conversation with yourself that is based on truth, love, and support to find solutions. Self-criticism closes the door to discuss solutions. This creates a barrier to change, leaving you stuck in old habits with only your own strength. Self-criticism disempowers and depletes you because it is not from God. Self-compassion opens a door for God's provision to be applied to your situation.

The compassion of God is powerful enough to transform us from death to life, to save our souls. To save our minds and lead us toward thoughts that bring life, overcoming, provision, and helpful behaviors and emotions. There has been a significant amount of research about how compassionately accepting ourselves and talking encouragingly to ourselves transforms our lives. We can lower our anxiety, stress, and depression and decrease the likelihood of reproducing past mistakes.

Self-compassion produces more kind behavior and compassion toward others. It appears to help provide perseverance, motivation, happiness, gratitude, emotional intelligence, and increased life satisfaction. In short, the research shows you may be empowered to imitate Christ in many areas of your life if you start by imitating His example of self-compassion. Deuteronomy 13:17 boldly declares that with compassion comes increase. Have some compassion on yourself today!

BUILDING YOUR PROSPEROUS MINDSET LIFE

Work to create a self-compassionate dialogue with yourself based on curiosity, kindness, hope, and commitment to change. Compassion helps you explore what happened and why. Criticism shuts down problem solving with judgment. When you are frustrated, sad, hurt, or angry, try the following:

1. Start by acknowledging it is okay and good to feel those emotions, even though they are uncomfortable. These are messages God enabled you to have to help you know there is something going on that you need to explore more.
2. Practice exploring the feeling by speaking or writing compassionately to yourself about the situation, as a good parent (even a TV or fictional parent) might speak to a child.
3. Accept and forgive yourself as you would a small child or best friend.
4. Small changes are more powerful and possible than perfection. Explore without judgment what you want or need to change, how you will change, and when and why you will change to reach a more prosperous life.

PROSPERITY PRAYER

Your compassion is my lifeline. Your compassion heals and empowers me. Your compassion gives me access to all I need, forgives me when I am wrong, and restores life and health to me. Help me to see the compassion You have for me in a greater way so that I can be more deeply transformed. Help me not think I know better than You what I deserve compassion for, as that holds me back from positive action in my life and in the world.

CREATING HOLISTIC PROSPERITY

 Relationships and Family: Compassion is a tool for increasing connecting points and relational investment and understanding.

 Spiritual: Compassion unlocks the heart of God in a situation.

 Health: Increasing your self-compassion leads to more stable emotions and better understanding your emotions. The ability to forgive yourself opens up doors of health to experience the healthy emotions of God.

 Financial: Helping others financially releases financial freedom and grace for yourself. It frees you from the love of money.

Professional: Having compassion on your bosses and coworkers and clients when they are having a bad day allows them to have the grace to have the same attitude toward you when you are having a difficult day.

 Social: Compassion is stopping to help others. Seeing the needs in your community and creating solutions to meet them makes your whole community stronger.

38

Word of Knowledge

And the Lord said to him, "Get up and go to the street called Straight, and inquire at the house of Judas for a man from Tarsus named Saul, for he is praying, and he has seen in a vision a man named Ananias come in and lay his hands on him, so that he might regain his sight."

—ACTS 9:11-12

The Bible says that the word of God helps discern the thoughts and intents of the heart. We can glean not only from the Logos Word of God but also from the Rhema word of God. The Logos is the written Word of God, the Bible. The Rhema word of God is the freshly spoken or uttered word of God. With applied spiritual, historical, and grammatical Logos understanding, we can pray and hear from God to receive the Rhema word of God for our own lives and the lives around us. God wants to speak to us; He has been talking to His kids for thousands of years!

God knows the count of all the hairs on our heads. He knows our cares, struggles, and desires. God knows it all. In an effort to distribute His heart and help humanity, He gave us a gift. It's called the word of knowledge. In a nutshell, God shares helpful facts about our pasts and presents to introduce victory, healing, breakthrough, and His perfect will to one of His children about someone else.

When we receive a word of knowledge, we receive God's mind and thoughts about a present and future person, place, or thing. It is both a spiritual gift and a wiring of our brains around how God thinks and what He knows. Have you received God's thoughts on your identity? Do you know who He has called you to be? What He has called you to do? Have you, like the disciples, been called but forgotten? Has disappointment or a feeling of disillusionment sent you backward into part of your old identity that is just not working for you? God wants to share facts about you to unlock your true potential.

I (Ally) was once given a word of knowledge from an unassuming older woman who said very specific things to me about my family and life and said with full assurance, "I feel like God says that you have a teaching and preaching anointing." I was just beginning to speak and teach, but this woman didn't have any way to know that about me with natural knowledge. I also did not feel particularly called to teaching or preaching. I was very shy as a child; in fact I was terrified of public speaking most of my life. However, this word of knowledge resonated with my heart and, over the years, with the help of God, I started to invest in that identity. I have now taught numerous groups, preached and presented, and spoken at many events. I rarely have any fear about it because it is who God made me to be.

Recently, both of us were praying with a woman about her life. I (Jeremy) asked God to share something important that might help her and unlock her potential. I heard a date from God! I said to her, "Does November 8 mean anything to you?" She said yes with a shocked look on her face. I said, "God doesn't want this date to be defining for you anymore. You are not called by this date, and God will redeem it." She started crying and shared that she received a cancer diagnosis on that date two years before. She lived in fear of cancer coming back, and that day has forever changed her life. I felt faith for her full recovery and shared it with her.

Now is the time to receive a fresh word of knowledge from God about your identity. He knows everything about you! He knows how you will thrive, what identity will make you prosper, and what identity is not yours and will feel like a burden. God wants to speak to you about your life to unlock your full potential. He wants to overlap your thoughts with His. We will abound in life when we carry the mindset that God knows, sees, and shares. Invite the gift of a word of knowledge today!

BUILDING YOUR PROSPEROUS MINDSET LIFE

Ask God to share His thoughts about your identity. Words of knowledge are a gift and a skill that God wants us to grow in. Like any skill, we need to practice. We can grow in words of knowledge through impartation, zeal, and prayer.

1. Ask the Lord for words of knowledge about your friends.

2. Ask questions that will unlock His heart about their cares, desires, hobbies, fears, and family.

3. Ask God what kingdom calling your friends might have and who they relate to most in the Bible. It will help you learn about their lives with one word from God.

4. Share these words with the person. No need to say "God says." Instead, start with, "I was thinking . . . ," "I feel . . . ," or "I wonder . . ." Use encouraging and friendly language.

PROSPERITY PRAYER

All knowledge is found in You, Jesus! Thank You, Jesus, that the Holy Spirit searches even the deepest parts of the Father in order to share them with us. We delight in Your knowledge that changes us, upgrades us, and sets us free. We love the gifts that You give. Thank You, Jesus, for distributing the gift of Your heart to us through words of knowledge. Bless you, Jesus. May Your gifts abound forever in us.

CREATING HOLISTIC PROSPERITY

Relationships and Family: Recognize that your thoughts about people may not be God's thoughts. Spend time in prayer pursuing His thoughts so you can be empowered to activate God's view of others and His plan for their lives.

Spiritual: Pursuing the active word of God unlocks our ability to perceive His voice, thoughts, and intentions. It empowers us to get closer to Him, to know He is near, and to make empowered decisions each day.

Health: One of the primary topics that people received words of knowledge about in the Bible was the topic of healing. Be open to God's thoughts on healing.

 Financial: God intimately knows your financial state and is your advocate to provide financial strategy and connections through words of knowledge.

 Professional: Some of the greatest professional upgrades happen from being in the right place at the right time to meet the right person. Following the prompting of the Holy Spirit about where you go and what you do increases your chances of greater connections and upgrades.

 Social: Words of knowledge provide awareness and opportunities to have a glimpse into others' futures and God's thoughts on the community, which allows for preparation, strategy, and solutions. It excites a group to work toward common goals.

39

New Structure

Nor do people put new wine into old wineskins; otherwise the wineskins burst, and the wine pours out and the wineskins are ruined; but they put new wine into fresh wineskins, and both are preserved.

—MATTHEW 9:17

I t's a funny idea: looking into our future, hoping things will change without any effort on our part. Something has to change to facilitate these new goals. It has been said that the definition of insanity is doing the same thing over and over again and expecting a different result. If we want different results, if we want to walk into a new season of our lives, we are often the ones who need to change. Our mindsets need to change. We may need to build a new structure to make way for new outcomes.

Recently married people know this well. When they were single, they each had certain ways of doing things, but after they got married their processes needed to change to accommodate another person. If someone wants to add on to their house, the city zoning board may ask them to install new foundation pillars to support the new infrastructure. If someone wants to eat healthier, they might need to buy different food and educate themselves on cooking healthier meals.

Let me tell you about a friend of ours. Her name is Maggie. She got a divorce after her husband cheated on her. It's now been seven years, and she hasn't started to date anyone. She is stuck in what once was, unable to move into her new season because her mindset is keeping her back. She is afraid of changing her thoughts because they feel familiar, but she also really wants to be in a relationship. The only way for Maggie to enter into the new season is for her to change her mindset about herself. She holds the keys to her life more than anyone else does. She can build a new world one thought at a time.

It is impossible to achieve new seasons of prosperity without a new structure or wineskin. In the Old Testament God stopped everything and introduced a new structure that forever changed history. He said, "Be sure that you make everything according to the pattern I have shown you here on the mountain" (Exodus 25:40 NLT). After that moment, the old pattern was gone and the world had a new structure. Jesus later fulfilled that pattern in person in meticulous fashion. The new structure that God introduced was a perfect picture of Jesus! This is how we introduce a new structure. We change the pattern from which we reproduce.

In our own lives, there are several psychological techniques that we can deploy in our mindsets to help us achieve new seasons and new structures of prosperity. We can use cognitive reframing, when we look to the good of a situation by framing it with a focus on positive, hopeful, meaningful possibilities instead of disappointments. This makes us feel invincible and emotionally healthy and strong. We can also think in shades of gray. Ask yourself, What is the third option here? instead of being so fixed on black-and-white answers. You may find that there are ten or twenty options for how to do something or how to move forward.

Let's get rid of our cognitive distortions and put forth new mindsets. Instead of black-and-white thinking, let's be open to new options. Instead of always discounting the positive, let's consider it all joy. Instead of mind reading in our relationships, let's open up paths of communication. God wants us to get rid of the old wineskin because it will burst if we receive new wine. The new wine will need to expand and mature in us. We are called to walk in the newness of life. To do so we will need new structures to carry what God has called us to.

BUILDING YOUR PROSPEROUS MINDSET LIFE

Trigger words or cognitive distortions almost always pull you down rather than building you up and strengthening you. They are often based in shame that is not from God. Three of these words are *should*, *never*, and *always*.

1. Create a list of five things you think you *should* be doing and are not. Things like, "I should be a better parent or partner" or "I should read my Bible more." Or create a list of five things you think will *never* change or will *always* be a certain way: "I will never be financially free" or "I will always be angry."

2. Take a moment to ask who says you *should* and who says you will *always* or *never*. If it is anyone other than God, you have caught a thinking error that is stealing life and energy from you.

3. Think of the exceptions and evidence that reveal the error for what it is. You can probably think of a time when you were a good parent or partner. When was a time you were not angry or when you were more financially free?

PROSPERITY PRAYER

Jesus, You are a perfect structure for my growth. As You usher me into new seasons of prosperity, break open my old wineskins that keep me from growing. Set me free from any cognitive dissonance. Lead me and guide me into new ways of thinking that promote long-term health and happiness. Thank You, Lord, for the patterns that You set in the mountains. Show us Your pattern today, Jesus. We look to You for these beautiful patterns to build from. Bless You, Jesus.

CREATING HOLISTIC PROSPERITY

 Relationships and Family: Developing boundaries with family members helps to create health and the ability to connect more genuinely, peacefully, and honestly in the future.

 Spiritual: Our spirits are renewed daily through connection with God. We should constantly be trying to restructure our spiritual walks and experiences to receive fully from God.

Health: In order to achieve the body and emotions you want, you may have to do away with old habits and activities and create new habits and activities that promote health.

 Financial: To achieve your spending goals you must assess costs and find ways to meet your goals with new structures.

 Professional: New professional structures may be simply creating a new work atmosphere that is life giving and productive. For example, change the offices of employees to be more effective based on personality meshes, distractors, and clashes. Or it might be moving one person to a different role or task that better fits their giftings.

 Social: New structures can be created through legislation and bills to bring about greater health in your community and area.

40

Possessing Promises

> *See, I have placed the land before you; go in and*
> *possess the land which the* LORD *swore to give to*
> *your fathers, to Abraham, to Isaac, and to Jacob,*
> *to them and their descendants after them.*
> —DEUTERONOMY 1:8

God wants us to know the rules of engagement. The best ones
are given in His promises. Then we know how we can connect
with God and what to expect from Him, and we can build our lives
around those hopes, dreams, and promises. There are thousands of
promises in the Bible. As we educate ourselves about them, we can
start to shape our own minds with those goals and promises because
we were made in God's image. Everything we discover about God is
ultimately a discovery about ourselves.

God has given us a beautiful blueprint for how to live the most prosperous life by giving us lives filled with promise. These promises are perfectly suited to fit the different facets of our lives. They cover everything from health to relationships, finances—you name it, everything! Now, we have two goals to tackle. First, we should educate ourselves on all the promises from the Father. Without vision, people perish (Proverbs 29:18 KJV). We need to know what the promises of God are so we are not ignorant of His blessing. Second, we need to grab hold of the promises and make them real, make them our own, and possess them.

This actionable progression should become a lifestyle goal of possessing the promises. The moment we realize a promise from God, others, or ourselves, we have the ability to obtain it. That is a "renewed" mind. "Let us hold tightly without wavering to the hope we affirm, for God can be trusted to keep his promise" (Hebrews 10:23 NLT). We can set our mind on the things above (Colossians 3:2) and bring forth the victory of fulfilled promises.

A renewed mind provides us with mindsets that help us take hold of the promises that are available as better options. A promise can lead us to the best-case scenario of the perfect will of God for our situation. What are God's promises that He has given you? How are you actively partnering with them through your mindsets? Yes, there is a promise of peace. Are you fully and actively possessing it? What about the promises of a prosperous family, health, everlasting life, safety, and abundance? How are you going after them? There are so many promises God has given, but we are not meant to be passive recipients in life. What has God promised you, and what is the plan you have to obtain it?

Promises are not just for when things are going well. They are also guideposts for our hearts and minds for when things are going south. They help anchor us during the storms of life. There was a time when someone let me (Jeremy) down in a monumental way. This letdown was huge. It affected everything I was doing. My emotions were shaken. My thoughts were running around as if in a hamster wheel. I could have stayed in this state of confusion and betrayal, but God brought to my remembrance all that Christ had promised. I accelerated my journey and overcame that setback because of the promises. I prayed, "God, You said I would be prosperous in this. This won't steal my emotions or time away. God, You are faithful to bring me through."

A renewed mind carries the promise of God and others in its thoughts daily. It keeps us from wandering situationally in the wilderness. The promised land is on the other side of what you are going through right now. Can you see it? Do you know how to get there? Hold fast to your promise. Pursue it until it becomes yours. In every situation you can find a promise to pursue.

BUILDING YOUR PROSPEROUS MINDSET LIFE

We must not believe that emotion is our God, our way, our truth, and our life. If we do, emotion becomes the focus of our lives and decisions, and it can mislead us. Sometimes feel-good emotions can mislead us if we do not recognize our logical and practical part in possessing the promise. Sometimes emotions like fear or discouragement can also derail us. Here is a process for assessing if emotional reasoning is sabotaging you and keeping you from reaching promises:

1. Know that getting messages through your emotions is good and a gift God created to help you bring resolution to situations. Emotions should be cared for as messengers but not worshiped as truth.

2. Identify who, where, or what the message is coming from. Is it coming from God, others, or yourself? This makes a big difference in helping you know what to do with the message.

3. Write out your thoughts and emotions and then compare your emotional reasoning with logical or spiritual reasoning.

4. To find logical reasoning, imagine a judge or lawyer is looking for cold, hard, concrete evidence that your emotions were telling the truth. Would he find anything? If not, or if he would find very little, this might mean your emotional reasoning on the topic is not fully trustworthy.

PROSPERITY PRAYER

God, You are the ultimate promise keeper. You are faithful and true and fulfill all Your promises. You watch over Your Word to make sure it performs itself. Thank You for being there for us. We will pursue Your promises with all of our hearts and create fulfilled promises with those around us. Show us how to go after and hold fast to all Your life-giving promises.

CREATING HOLISTIC PROSPERITY

 Relationships and Family: Just as we are called to possess promises, we must fulfill the promises we offer, or our relationships will not prosper. Ask others if they feel there are promises you have not fulfilled; hear them and contemplate what God would have you do.

Spiritual: Think about the hundreds of available biblical promises. As Christians we have the birthright that gives us the ability to grab hold of them and claim them as our own if we pursue them with God.

 Health: "For God has not given us a spirit of fear, but . . . of a sound mind" (2 Timothy 1:7 NKJV). To possess this promise, we have to partner with God and seek practical tools to help our minds be sound.

 Financial: God wants to share financial promises and goals with you each year. You can have an open mind to work in partnership with God to bring about the financial promise in various creative ways. Ask God how much you should make next year.

 Professional: If someone is following through on their promise to perform a service or provide a product, and they fulfill that promise in a beautiful and timely manner, they will see an increase in repeat customers as well as new customers.

 Social: What are the promises God has given over your region, city, or community? You can work to create opportunities to lead your city and community into those promises.

41

Forgiveness

And forgive us our debts, as we also have forgiven our debtors.

—MATTHEW 6:12

The power of the cross is mind-blowing. We all know that Jesus, being perfect in all ways, came to the earth to forgive our sin and show us the way of life. Through the cross Jesus not only made a way to release forgiveness but for us to forgive as well. This is incredible! One of the first transferable elements to salvation was our ability to forgive sin. How could we possibly forgive someone else's sin unless we have access to the power of the cross in us? We do, and it is called salvation.

"And whenever you stand praying, forgive, if you have anything against anyone, so that your Father also who is in heaven may for-give you your trespasses" (Mark 11:25 ESV). Forgiveness is a divine principle. It is a cognitive process that involves others, but it mostly involves yourself. Unforgiveness ties you to something that is not good, something that was hurtful or did not empower you. It keeps your mind closed to new options because you are so busy hanging onto the past, a wrong, and the negative. We fail to look for God's redemption. Most people think forgiveness is about releasing others, but it is actually about properly restoring yourself.

Training your mind to forgive is not about the other person. It's about your freedom. It means you are freeing yourself from anxi-ety, depression, stress, fear, and anger caused by another. Mistakes and sin are not the same thing. Forgiveness is available for both, and love covers a multitude of sins. We cannot give what we have not received first. We need to receive an exchange from God and extend to both ourselves and the people around us His supernatural gift and power of forgiveness. Then we can restore ourselves to a pre-wronged state and also forgive the sins of others. We now have authority to release ourselves and the people around us from the bondage of sin.

"Forgive and forget" is a phrase that is often misunderstood. After getting the emotional message of being wronged, you should work to resolve the feelings and free yourself from them. This frees you from the emotional impact of the wrong. Then yes, maybe forget about living in the feelings, forget the anger, forget feeling wronged. But it is important to be aware that people are showing you who they are. Your forgiveness extends a possibility to them for transforma-tion, restoration, and health, but they do not have to accept it. Nor will they always take it in a way that allows them to be transformed by it. We should be aware of who they are and not expect them to change without evidence of that change.

Many people struggle the most to forgive themselves, which is the biggest disservice they could do to themselves and those they love. This mindset of unforgiveness impacts relationships. A common example is parents who did the best they could at the time but struggle to forgive themselves for their mistakes raising their child. This mindset of unforgiveness continues to color and possibly hurt the relationship. The parents bring underlying shame and pressure to try to make it up to the child or to themselves.

You have been given the gift to forgive, to free yourself. If your mind is set on releasing people from their transgressions, you will keep in good standing with God because He released you of all your transgressions against Him. As we enter into forgiveness ourselves, we will realize that being debt free is living our best life. We will give the gift of the cancellation of debt to those around us. We will truly prosper if we hold fast to this.

BUILDING YOUR PROSPEROUS MINDSET LIFE

What unforgiveness is holding you back from prosperity today?

1. Take a moment to think and pray about someone you may not have fully forgiven. Remember, this might be yourself.
2. Embrace the freedom of forgiveness today, and breathe in the relief of not being qualified or required to be judge and jury and jailer to the emotions about the wrong.
3. Let the toxicity go and imagine it leaving your heart, mind, home, and family.
4. What do you see on the other side of forgiveness that you have not had access to before? If the wrong never happened or was restored, what would be different?
5. Now live according to that mindset and heart space.

PROSPERITY PRAYER

Jesus, thank You for the gift of forgiveness. You are a wonderful God. We love what forgiveness has to offer and invite it into our lives daily. Captivate our hearts with the power of love and teach us to extend forgiveness to ourselves and to those around us. We want to be debt free concerning our transgressions and free concerning those around us. Thank You, God, for this power.

CREATING HOLISTIC PROSPERITY

 Relationships and Family: Forgiveness enables you to have full joy about anything your family has given you, even if it was only life itself. It frees you to pursue ways to get unmet needs fulfilled in other ways and to love without being held back by your own hurt.

 Spiritual: Forgiveness allows us to relate to Jesus and the Father and to be able to see our life, hope, and joy more freely.

 Health: Forgiving yourself for your mistakes and accepting God's forgiveness is essential to prospering in your emotions. He knew this, which is why He made such a point to tell us we are forgiven. Unforgiveness is the gateway for so many unhealthy characteristics—stress, anxiety, fear, panic, loneliness—and habits that negatively impact your health.

 Financial: Repent and change bad mindsets that are bringing destructive habits in spending.

Professional: Forgiveness is a relational experience that begins to repair important relationships to keep a team strong and productive together at work. Forgiving is key to resolving and solving problems.

 Social: Our communities suffer when there is unforgiveness and a lack of asking for forgiveness. Part of how we bring prosperity to our communities is by humbly asking forgiveness for wrongs done against other communities, even in the past.

42

Identity

He predestined us to adoption as sons through Jesus Christ to Himself, according to the kind intention of His will, to the praise of the glory of His grace, which He freely bestowed on us in the Beloved. In Him we have redemption through His blood, the forgiveness of our trespasses, according to the riches of His grace which He lavished on us.

—EPHESIANS 1:5–8

Identity is the internal anchor for who we are and what we do. The Bible is filled with people whose identity was firmly rooted and grounded in God, even to the point of death. Daniel's identity was so strong that he did what was right even though he was thrown in the lion's den for it. As Christians, our identities are rooted in Christ. Our identities are our thoughts and the feedback that we accept from others or ourselves. We have a measure of power to define our own identities based on our values, belief systems, vision, and mission. "As [a man] thinks in his heart, so is he" (Proverbs 23:7 NKJV).

Those with the strongest identity have acknowledged their values and act according to them most of the time. They know their values hierarchy and do a few things they value greatly rather than many things they don't value very much. Our thought process builds the framework for our mission, vision, and values. This, in turn, helps us to be strong and stable in the face of both challenges and success. Identity brings clarity, vision, and hope—what to do and why you want to do it. We all have to go through a process of trusting ourselves to get to the point of a strong and sure identity. Without tests, our identity is only a nice idea without any long-term impact.

Imagine you have a friend who comes to talk to you, saying he feels lost in life. Maybe you have noticed changes in him over the years but never addressed it. This person does not seem to have the same enthusiasm, the same spark in life. The friend comes to you and says that since he started a dating relationship, he has changed. He started to take on the values of the person he was dating and lost his sense of who he was. He took a job he thought the person he was dating would like him to take, but it is a job that he does not value or enjoy. The impact of this can be deep when it comes to prosperity. Why? Because he is living in conflict with his internal values and identity. If our values are not congruent with who we know ourselves to be, we will likely lose joy, happiness, and meaning in life.

Our identity may be built around many things—our culture, where we live, what we do, how we act or think. Those with a strong identity have great benefits. They have internal strength, peace, clarity, and direction. When you know who you are, you are not vulnerable to what others think and the negative thoughts in your head. You can put up boundaries to assert what is true about yourself in a way that is powerful, not full of fear or striving or manipulation.

In contrast, without a strong identity you will spend days, months, and years in high stress, trying to control what others think about you. A challenge with knowing your identity comes from a lack of boundaries with others' thoughts about who you are as well as your own thoughts about who you are. The real challenge is to proactively develop what you think about you instead of trying to control the people and places on the outside of you. When you control your thoughts and mindset about yourself, you can have healthy boundaries and relationships with others. Unless you work to accept and like yourself, you will always try to control others' thoughts and feelings about you as a form of essential protection. But trying to control others leads to exhaustion, frustration, loneliness, anxiety, abandonment, and burnout.

When you know who you are, others feel they do too. They are more likely to want to be around you and trust you. What we believe to be true about ourselves is important because not accepting God's truth about us and having boundaries to say no to another identity often drives self-sabotage. If our identity is based on abandonment, fear of loss, and self-protection, our mind will work to recreate those things. Our thoughts about our identity are demonstrated through our actions and situations in life. Identity as a child of God allows us to not react but come from a sturdy place of knowing who we are.

BUILDING YOUR PROSPEROUS MINDSET LIFE

Consider an area of your life where you are doing something only to make others happy. These are life-draining activities and, if you have too many, you cannot walk out your identity. Notice when you start to worry about or think about what others think. Here are a few steps to take when that happens:

- Choose to ask yourself what you think based on your values. This is an important switch to make. To have a strong identity you must develop trust with yourself.
- Spend time exploring the Bible to find and define what God's identity is for you. You are created in His image and alive in Christ. Practice saying no to thoughts or opinions that say otherwise.
- Say yes and no to requests. A sure sign of opportunity to build your identity is if you feel stress and anxiety when you have to say no. Jesus said both yes and no to requests very easily, and when you have identity, you can too.
- Continue to consider your values and whether your behaviors line up with your values. If not, why? What are the things that make you vulnerable to losing your sense of self? Brainstorm ways to strengthen yourself in this area or ask friends and family for ideas.

PROSPERITY PRAYER

God, You have the strongest identity of any person we know. You are the Anchor for all of us to live and to look toward. Thank You for giving us the identity of your Son. The loving nature of who You are brings forth the statutes and structure of heaven for us to become the best versions of ourselves. Thank You for modeling for us the best identity.

CREATING HOLISTIC PROSPERITY

 Relationships and Family: If your relationships are strong, it is more likely that your sense of identity will be strong as well.

 Spiritual: What God says about your identity is the single most important thing that you should believe about who you are and what you can do. Your identity is formed when you understand who you are in Christ, not in your own strength.

 Health: Building a strong identity leads you to automatically start to make or accept decisions that are in line with your identity. As you change your feelings about who you are to be positive, positive behaviors will follow.

 Financial: Our finances paint a picture about who we are. How we spend money tells us a lot about how we think of ourselves. To change your finances, you have to be willing to change your perspective about who you are and how valuable you are without any fancy clothes, titles, jobs, cars, or other things.

 Professional: Continue to invest in your professional identity, learning new skills to morph your identity and elevate your professional position.

 Social: The groups we are a part of say a lot about who we think we are and where we feel we belong in the world.

PART 7

Increasing Social Prosperity

Scripture is clear: we are made to live in community. We all have a part to play not just in our close relationships with family and friends but in our social circles, our society, and our world. Those with strong communities tend to be happier and more fulfilled. This may look different for every person, but how can we cultivate community practically? We cannot just pray for it; we need to practice skills that help us to put action behind our prayer and create a strong, prospering community. Our social circles will assist us in our goals and dreams. When a vibrant community tackles projects like inclusion, hunger, and social justice, progress can be made. We can shape our world through powerful communities creating change for good.

43

Giving to the Poor

Give, and it will be given to you. They will pour into your lap a good measure—pressed down, shaken together, and running over. For by your standard of measure it will be measured to you in return.

—LUKE 6:38

Some of God's heavenly mandates are instilled in our prosperous journeys not only to help us but to help those around us. For example, helping us socially in our communities, in our churches, and in our regions. To the natural mind, giving doesn't sound like the best thing to do when you are trying to build wealth. However, if giving to the poor opened up a spiritual door to more prosperity in your walk with God, it would be the easiest thing to do.

Our Father in heaven is very clever, and in His cleverness He instilled a reward for us if we take care of those He loves. Proverbs 19:17 says, "Whoever is kind to the poor lends to the LORD, and he will reward them for what they have done" (NIV). This reward is based on principle and each act of generosity. God is doubling down on all humanity to ensure its connectedness and long-term success, all the while breaking down social, racial, and socioeconomic barriers. He loves all of us and wants us all to succeed.

We love how Jesus put Himself at the center of the act of giving. He wants us to think of Him and emotionally connect with His heart when we give to the poor. When we notice someone poor on the street and we stop to connect with Jesus' heart about them, we grow in connection to God's will (what He is thinking, feeling, and doing) and align ourselves for the most prosperous journey. What a beautiful opportunity.

Both of us are big foodies, and one of our favorite chefs is José Andrés. We love his food, but we also eat at his restaurants because we appreciate that he gives a tremendous amount of time, energy, and finances to the poor through an organization called World Central Kitchen. This organization has the goal of providing smart solutions to hunger and poverty. It provides millions of freshly made, nutritious meals around the world as emergency food relief and through long-term programs. We feel that as we eat at his restaurants, in some small way, we are helping the poor and giving to God's heart.

Socially conscious businesses have been on the rise and have become attractive to our generation much like in the example we just shared. How many other people eat at José Andrés's restaurants for the same reasons? We think there are a lot. Communities, churches, and companies are also turning to social justice issues related to the poor through galas, fundraisers, and product-centric initiatives. It is an attractive and helpful rallying call. This kind of generosity opens up cities and grows businesses.

We all have the unique invitation to align with God's values and get blessed in the meantime. How do we prosper when we give to the poor? We become happier people when we give. Our overall happiness is tied to our ability to give, not to receive. Also, Jesus rewards us in ways we cannot even measure. When we give, it will be given back to us at God's ROI rates.

BUILDING YOUR PROSPEROUS SOCIAL LIFE

From the perspective of holistic prosperity, one might argue that some of poorest in the world are the people who feel disconnected, unloved, and unhappy. Instead of looking at them with frustration and disdain, spending time with them can help you acquire a better perspective of how much you have. Whatever you give to the least of them, you give to Jesus. Who do you know who might need emotional strength and encouragement today? Here are some ways to give:

- Write a letter of encouragement.
- Surprise the person with flowers or a gift.
- Offer to help with yard work, watch the person's kids for a few hours, or make a meal.
- Simply spend time with the person—watch a movie, play a game, put together a picnic.
- Show curiosity and interest in the person's life.
- Ask him or her out to coffee or lunch and pay for it.

PROSPERITY PRAYER

You are the ultimate Giver. You gave us all we have: the world, the sun, people. Most of all, You give us Yourself. You freely offer Yourself, Your resources, Your peace, Your love, Your joy, and You always have enough. You never run out, and as You give, nothing is taken away from You. You are my role model. Help me think like You.

CREATING HOLISTIC PROSPERITY

 Relationships and Family: When you give to the poor together with your family, you increase bonding and relational connection. You feel like you are on the same team, you are reaching goals together, and you are sharing meaningful experiences.

 Spiritual: Giving to the poor helps to align your thoughts and mind to see with the eyes of God and be His hands and feet to the world.

 Health: Giving to the poor helps you emotionally as you recognize the privileges and things that you have and experience the positive emotions of being able to make a difference to someone. It also lowers cortisol and stress levels, giving you a healthier body.

 Financial: Giving to the poor is like lending to God. He will repay. Not only that, giving to the poor is one way to prevent selfishness and possessiveness over your finances, opening the door for more to be given to you.

Professional: Giving to the poor increases your social connections when you attend events or social activities based around giving. This could be a fundraising walk or a gala. Either way, you put yourself in a place to meet connections that can further your professional life.

 Mindset: Giving to the poor allows you to see the world through God's eyes and see yourself more clearly. You are freed of negative mindsets like hopelessness when you give hope to others. You are freed from the mindsets of greed and selfishness when you take the time to consider the needs of others.

44

Pruning

Every branch in Me that does not bear fruit, He
takes away; and every branch that bears fruit, He
prunes it so that it may bear more fruit.
—JOHN 15:2

God is a gardener and therefore so are we. He is deeply connected to what we need to thrive. God wants to prune and cut away all things that are not leading us to an abundant life. Pruning brings health, greater quality, and overall longevity. It is there so that ultimately we can produce and maintain more good fruit in our lives. This invitation comes from John 15:2: "He prunes it so that it may bear more fruit."

Pruning can be applied to every area of life, especially to our social circles. Many of us may find ourselves overcommitted to people, things, or communities that drain our overall vitality. Sometimes these are good things that empower us, but we still need to cut back to make room for new growth in the next season. Sometimes we have to cut off things that are not healthy or producing life. We are never our best when we are overextended or hanging on to dead weight. It may feel like cutting back overgrowth or dead things is not the right thing to do in the moment, but it will keep us from our full potential if we don't embrace it.

We must open ourselves up to the possibilities of the best and be willing to prune anything that gets in the way. God pruned Gideon's army in the Old Testament (Judges 7). God pruned humanity with Noah's ark. Saying no, cutting back, and cutting off are part of a powerful boundary. Jesus said no to a lot of things. That is why He completed what God called Him to do. He would not have been able to do that by saying yes to every request.

I (Jeremy) experienced a season of transition a few years back with my social circle, friends, and community. A good friend of mine once shared many of my values, but then he started hanging out with the wrong crowd. This friend started consuming drugs and alcohol daily. His life was changing for the worse, and his circles of friends were divided over the issue. Half of them felt like breaking free of the person and letting him just live his life. The other half did not care about their drug-induced friend's new lifestyle as much and wanted to keep hanging out with him. I prayed and consulted with others not connected to the matter. I did not feel that God was calling me to minister to the person and continue connection but that I needed to allow others to do so. I felt it was best to cut off the relationship because it was becoming toxic. In doing so, I opened up my time, energy, and heart to relationships that gave me abundant life and were reciprocal in nature.

We can partner with God in pruning our social circles if they do not align with our value systems. It is good to be friends with people who may not share all your values, but you may enjoy and prosper in your social life more if you also spend time with people who do. There are a few ways to check if pruning would be a good thing. First, do you want to be more like the person or group you are spending time with? On a neurological level, we become like the people we spend time with. We start to think differently, talk differently, and do different things. Second, how do you feel around your friends? Prune out people that constantly say and do things to make you feel bad about yourself. Third, do an assessment of what God's purpose is for a relationship. If you find that you are spending a lot of time in a relationship that doesn't serve God's purposes, adjust the amount of time you spend with that person. Make plenty of room for other relationships that motivate you, drive you, and serve the purposes God has for you.

BUILDING YOUR PROSPEROUS SOCIAL LIFE

Choose one or more of the following options to start pruning your life for abundance today:

- Practice saying no to an event, an invitation, or a gathering that is not part of your calling and you do not feel gives you life.
- Prune your home or environment. Clean out cupboards and closets in a room and donate or throw out the old to have a more prosperous, clutter-free, relaxing environment.
- Practice saying no to a person or friend. Explore any fears you might have about saying no to them or how you might stay connected to them despite a disagreement.
- Create a list of ten things you feel pressure to do. Rate them in order of importance. Invite God to give you perspective so you can prune off the least important things.

PROSPERITY PRAYER

God, You are the best Gardener. You till the soil of our hearts, plant seeds of righteousness, and cut out every dead thing that will keep us from our growth potential. Thank You for watching over us so well. God, we give You full permission to cut back any area that keeps us from Your love. Cut it off to save us and comfort us when it hurts. We lean on You in our times of victory and pruning. You are such a loving Father.

CREATING HOLISTIC PROSPERITY

 Relationships and Family: Cut back on activities or conversations that stress your relationships with your family.

 Spiritual: Be open to the idea of God cutting back things in your heart that you are familiar with, in order for you to grow.

 Health: Cut back music, movies, and food that are not serving long-term health goals. Cut back on things that cause your time to be unproductive.

 Financial: Take stock of your expenses and your budget. Look at subscriptions or other purchases that are not producing fruit in your life.

 Professional: Prune activities that are not producing good fruit or have not led to good increase for some time.

Mindset: Take your thoughts captive, say no, and remove thoughts that do not lead to an abundant life, flourishing, and constructive beliefs about yourself.

45

Rest

*For he said to Judah, "Let us build these cities
and surround them with walls and towers, gates
and bars. The land is still ours because we have
sought the LORD our God; we have sought Him,
and He has given us rest on every side." So they
built and prospered.*

—2 CHRONICLES 14:7

S ome may think it's counterintuitive to think about prosperity
being connected to rest, but it's true in more ways than one.
Rest is multidimensional. Out of rest we prosper. In rest we prosper.
The reward of rest is prosperity. Naturally, rest is situational, and,
as we rest, our bodies and minds have time to recover. Rest is also

spiritual; Jesus supplies us with the reward of the cross through His peace and rest.

In the beginning, God rested from all His creative works on the seventh day. He did not do this because He was tired. That is a silly thought. God got tired after creating the heavens and the earth? He needed a nap? No way! God was showing us what we needed. He was showing us and modeling for us a day of rest from all our works, a Sabbath. That is why Jesus declared that He is the Lord of the Sabbath.

God is not religious about rest; our bodies are wired to rest. We should extend this rest into our social spheres and introduce the rewards of rest to our communities, churches, and friends. One of the best ways to socially build is through play! Rest does not mean that you are lying in bed all day doing nothing. Rest can be anything that is not work. It can be activities, recreational sports, reading a book, or watching a movie.

Spending time together without stress allows our brains to calibrate and enables us to bond. It helps us to feel known, as rest brings vulnerability when our walls are not up and we are in a state of relaxation. Our quality time is magnified when we introduce rest to our social circles because when we are agenda-free, we feel connected and loved. People with agendas leave when it is time to rest. Relationships take on a different pace, and quality comes forth. That is why weekends and vacations are so rest oriented.

Social bonding increases with rest. Needs and wants are brought forth, and the resolution of pain and challenges comes about. Therefore church events are important to build a community and relationships. This is one big reason that we celebrate holidays as a community. This is why better deals are made when we take a client out to eat or take our boss out to golf.

God wants us to prosper and created us to have better relationships, build better communities, and strengthen our social networks when we come from a place of rest, maintain a place of rest, and work from rest. Hebrews 4:11 says we should strive to enter into the rest of the Lord.

BUILDING YOUR PROSPEROUS SOCIAL LIFE

Plan a social event with friends—or even one-on-one time with someone—that revolves around the idea of resting. Invite those people who help you feel most rested internally and with whom you do not feel you have to perform. The point is to create the atmosphere for bonding to take place. Imagine how it would change your life if you knew you had a day every month set apart for time to rest with friends. Here are some ideas:

- Play games to create a sense of teamwork, trust, and comradery that can translate into other areas of your life and friendships.
- Work on a project or craft that will enrich your lives.
- Choose a book and read out loud to one another.
- Get together and focus on any area of interest you share that is not work.

PROSPERITY PRAYER

It is Your delight to give us rest, Jesus. Thank You for the reward of the cross. We are so thankful for the blessing of Your payment. We are at home in Your rest. Send out Your favor and provide us rest on every side. Do not let the armies come at us. We abide in You. We thrive in You. Thank You, Jesus, for loving us so much.

CREATING HOLISTIC PROSPERITY

 Relationships and Family: Creating places, time, and space for the people closest to us to rest empowers them to be refreshed and bring their best into the relationship.

 Spiritual: The ultimate reward of the cross is rest. Our spiritual inheritance is for us to enter into rest and peace. Getting to know the Father provides us with spiritual rest.

 Health: The benefits of rest are drastic and empowering. We experience our best feelings when we are in a place of rest and practice rest often.

 Financial: If we are diligent to create a sense of peace and rest with our finances, we will make better financial decisions. Feeling nervous or stressed about finances often leads to making impulsive or reactionary decisions that sabotage success.

 Professional: Performance, stamina, problem solving, and emotional stability all impact our careers. All these areas are directly affected by our level of rest.

 Mindset: Develop the skill of entering into thoughts of peace and rest no matter where you are or what you are doing. With practice, rest is always an option. We can control our mindset in any situation and experience stability and peace.

46

Signs

> This, the first of his signs, Jesus did at Cana in Galilee, and manifested his glory. And his disciples believed in him.
>
> **—JOHN 2:11 ESV**

e are all looking for direction on what to do, where to go, and who to hang out with. Big and small indicators help us with this in natural and spiritual ways. These indicators are called signs. We can find signs in everything, including God. One of God's primary languages is signs.

Signs from our bodies, from our social spheres, and from God should all be communicating something to us. Like any relationship, we need to take the time to understand what the signs are saying. To understand them we use our past, present, and future expectations to form our lens through which we interpret the signs. This frame of reference can be established with God as well. We have been given a natural and supernatural process for signs.

Signs may be natural or supernatural in character, but they are all communicators meant to bring clarity and better understanding. When trying to make sense of a relationship that has gone wrong, people often say, "I never saw the signs." Being aware of the social signs we receive helps us to prosper in those relationships and understand what those relationships may require to reach the next level. What are the indicators that tell us if we are going down the right path? It's important that we learn to recognize the signs and act on them.

Jesus was ushered in with signs to lead His children and consistently showed off signs to communities so He could lead them. Socially, signs help to lead multitudes of people—that is why God introduced signs and wonders in the church. We may miss the signs if we struggle to see from others' perspectives. Building social intelligence is key to not missing the signs. This process starts with empathy—that is, the ability to put ourselves in the shoes of others. Many did not see the signs of Jesus that were clearly laid out. Those whose eyes were open to see the signs could prosper. Those who were blinded by their perception and belief that Jesus would come as a ruling dictator missed the signs.

When we look only from our own perspectives, we will spend a lot of time missing the signs displayed around us. We will spend a lot of time defending our positions and in conflict instead of in communication and unity. We are more likely to achieve goals as a community when we can recognize the signs of the needs, values, and expectations of others. When we do this, we can find out what is needed. Leaders are often put in a position to see the signs for their communities. God may be giving them dreams. They may be led by a particular verse or message they hear. These indicators could be clear messages naturally or spiritually.

The way we start to read social signs is by recognizing that everyone sees things differently based on their upbringing, past, and experience. We are driven by what we expect or hope for. As we train our senses to discern between good and evil, we will also cultivate our ability to detect signs to lead us and those in our social networks to paths of prosperity. Discernment is a key partner in identifying and walking in the signs for our present time.

BUILDING YOUR PROSPEROUS SOCIAL LIFE

Discerning signs in social settings depends on developing emotional intelligence and the ability to understand others' perspectives. Here are some steps that might help:

1. Assume that people will see most things at least somewhat differently than you do.
2. Be curious about what others say and do. Drop any assumption that you know what they mean when they say things (especially things you find frustrating).
3. Recognize that their perspective may be helpful for them in some way, even if it is not a fully accurate viewpoint. Be willing to put yourself in their shoes and wonder why they hold that perspective.
4. Be aware of body language, tone of voice, and other signs. What does the person's body language communicate?
5. Ask! The greatest way to see if you are reading signs correctly is by checking in regularly, especially when you feel something is off.

279

PROSPERITY PRAYER

God, You are a sign and a wonder. We look up to You in the heavens for signs of where You are in our lives today. Lead us like the North Star that professed the coming of Jesus. We thank You for being such a wonderful guide to us. We love when You lead us into ways of righteousness. Thank You, God, for always being there as our partner. We love You.

CREATING HOLISTIC PROSPERITY

 Relationships and Family: Pick up on signs from family and friends. Get to know the signs when things are going well and the signs when things are not going well. Notice three things a person does, the way he or she talks, and so forth. Whether the person is doing well or having a bad day, pick up on the signs to better connect with them.

 Spiritual: God's first love language is to speak to us through signs and symbols in parables.

 Health: Your emotions are signs of bigger things going on. Be aware of them and what they are communicating. Your body will manifest signs of sickness to alert you. Pay attention to your body and the signs of frustration it may be telling you to resolve, which can help prevent your emotions from building up.

Financial: Track your personal profit and losses each month. Notice trends of when you are likely to spend more or purchase impulsively. Your numbers will always tell a truthful story; they will not lie.

 Professional: Pay attention to signs that you may no longer be a good fit for your job or for working with a certain client. For example, you might feel increasingly burned out or tired at work, you may find yourself increasingly in the middle of tense conversations, or you may feel a lack of meaning and purpose in your job.

 Mindset: Thoughts of anxiety that don't lead to action or next steps are often signs that something might be wrong in the way you are thinking about God, yourself, or your future. Check in with your thoughts. There are always signs to help lead and guide us. We need to be looking for them.

47

Looking Forward

Remember not the former things,
nor consider the things of old.
Behold, I am doing a new thing;
now it springs forth, do you not perceive it?
I will make a way in the wilderness
and rivers in the desert.

—ISAIAH 43:18–19 ESV

God wants us to look forward. Many times throughout the Bible He called people to leave things behind and not look back. Lot, Abraham, the rich young ruler, and the disciples are examples. The people of Israel got themselves into trouble and wandered in the wilderness. Partly, this was exacerbated because they looked back to how life had been before they escaped captivity and started to compare their present life in a very toxic way. This led to grumbling and frustration.

Looking forward socially creates a lane for us to be healthy. If we are only looking back on what we did and didn't do, it does not always lead to fullness of hope or joy. In fact, when we stop looking and moving forward as a business, community, or church, we are going to stagnate or go backward. Looking forward means we have hope, and hope has energy to propel us forward.

Viktor Frankl was a psychologist forced into a concentration camp during World War II. He said when he paid attention, he could start to identify who would not make it out of the camp alive. When someone stopped talking about or hoping for a good future, they were not able to even consider a way forward after such tragedy. He said he trained his mind to focus on and imagine life ahead as good, hopeful, and full of meaning. He started to find purpose in observing the behavior of those around him. As a psychologist he planned how he would use this information to teach powerful lessons later, when the war was over. Despite enduring horrific conditions and despite losing his beloved wife and other family members, he was able to survive and later thrive because he developed the skill of looking forward.

One way we look forward is by connecting with our meaning and purpose. It increases bonding, unity, trust, and connection. Often we see this in sports teams that work together toward a common goal. People are happier working in unity than working toward different goals. While looking forward together, there is an instilled hope and pleasure of what is to come. Those who cannot look forward together with joy and hope will likely not move forward together for long. Building together can be a rewarding process of seeing what is possible and moving into that by using the gifts of different people in the community to make a goal into reality.

We love to plan travel together with friends because it is very rewarding to look into the future and plan fun, memorable moments. One time, I (Jeremy) was planning a trip for Ally and realized if I did not share the details, it would rob Ally of the joy of planning, dreaming, and hoping. Inviting people into the process versus just inviting them into the destination is socially important and something we both love to do. That creates just as much long-term satisfaction as actually being there.

Socially, we all have a future. Our churches, communities, small groups, and social spheres all have something to look forward to. As we become good planners and communicators, our communities will grab hold of the vision and run together. We can all dream together into our new season of prosperity. Let's give our friends a clear message of hope to look forward to this year.

BUILDING YOUR PROSPEROUS SOCIAL LIFE

Make sure you have something on the calendar you are looking forward to with friends. Instead of planning several little things, sometimes it is more fun to plan something bigger but very meaningful or exciting to you.

- What social things are you currently looking forward to? Imagine them in your mind: What will you feel like, what will you wear, what will you eat, who will you see, and how will you think about yourself?
- How might you plan or suggest something that your community or group can look forward to? It could be an outreach, a special dinner, a project, or a vacation.
- For others in your community, it may be hard for them to

participate. You can still offer them the gift of meaning, time, and connection that they can look forward to by sharing with them when you are planning to visit or call them.

PROSPERITY PRAYER

Jesus, uncap the dreamer in us. We want to dream, plan, and strategize all of our wonderful things to look forward to. You are such a visionary and place rewards ahead of us so we can see and realize what is possible. Thank You for training us this way. We love You, Jesus. Help us to look forward to all that You have called us to so we can realize it one day soon.

CREATING HOLISTIC PROSPERITY

 Relationships and Family: A great investment in future endeavors is to instill a future activity, dream, or goal into the present situation with your friends and family that you can look forward to together.

 Spiritual: God asks us to "be still, and know that I am God" (Psalm 46:10 NIV). God is more interested in spending time with us than we are with Him. He wants to reveal Himself as we spend time connecting with Him. When we are still, we get to know Him and the revelation of who He is.

Health: Setting a goal gives us a target we can look forward to and a model of an example of health. Setting goals with our health and being aware of people who have what we want to become is important. It helps us see how to close the gap between who we are and who we want to become.

 Financial: We need to set attainable targets. Budgets allow us to be comfortable with our lives. We can look forward to knowing our realistic financial scenario. We can look forward to how we can spend extra money, how we can donate, and so on.

 Professional: It is powerful to give your employees a deposit of what could be, how they can look forward to growing with your company, and the rewards of growing with your company. Without vision for how a job can better their futures, employees will look elsewhere.

 Mindset: Our mindset increases our strength and power to persevere through hard times. Jesus persevered for the joy set before Him because He was looking forward to the reward. Look forward and see how a hard situation, interaction, or season can benefit you in the future.

48

Sowing

Remember this: Whoever sows sparingly will also reap sparingly, and whoever sows generously will also reap generously. Each of you should give what you have decided in your heart to give, not reluctantly or under compulsion, for God loves a cheerful giver. And God is able to bless you abundantly, so that in all things at all times, having all that you need, you will abound in every good work.

—2 Corinthians 9:6–8 NIV

Most of us know and love the idea of sowing. It is a farming term that alludes to the planting of seeds. God is a farmer at heart, and He loves the process. We should glean from this analogy to bring us into a full understanding of what sowing actually means and what goes into it. When we introduce people to the miracles and transformational power of God, it gives us a sense of what the Spirit can do. God can move fast, He can work miracles, and nothing is in His way. He is a God of process as well, however, and so are we because we were made in His image.

Sowing is an intentional process of planting one seed at a time and committing to the legacy of what it could bring. Sowing is an investment before expecting to receive anything. It postures us for a natural, easy progression into our promises instead of superstar progression or overnight success. Plant and be faithful to nurture, water, and tend to your garden. Trust the process! "The wicked man earns an empty wage, but he who sows righteousness reaps a true reward" (Proverbs 11:18 BSB). If we try to cheat the process, we will get nothing.

We can incorporate sowing into every area of life but especially into our social spheres. We can sow into our communities by incorporating small acts of kindness. We can sow time, energy, and care by preferring others and building others up—not by pushing ahead for ourselves but bringing others up to our level, as did Jesus. He became a servant of all and planted seeds of righteousness in others so the seeds would bloom into a full harvest. Relationships are like fields we prepare for harvest. Have we planted enough seeds to bring forth the yield we expect in our relationships?

Relationships of any kind do not happen overnight. My (Ally's) grandmother was sowing into her community from the moment she moved there in her early twenties. If anything needed to be done, she would do it, no matter how glamorous or unglamorous. For a time, she was called "the trash lady of Hermosa Beach" for starting an initiative to get the first trash cans placed around the city. She volunteered at the women's club and the garden club, she was the first female member of the Hermosa Beach Kiwanis Club, and more.

She sowed selflessly with genuine interest in, care for, and encouragement for others. So, when others saw her, they just wanted to be around her, to work with her, to support her initiatives. Whenever she needed support in anything, it was there, because she had already sown it. This also carried over into her professional life and connections. She is an incredible example of someone who was faithful in the process. She didn't try to get fancy and impatiently rush things.

"And those are the ones on whom seed was sown on the good soil; and they hear the word and accept it and bear fruit, thirty, sixty, and a hundredfold" (Mark 4:20). Your yield is set based on your ability to plant the seeds that you are given. Sometimes people get greedy and sloppy with the seeds they are given, and they eat them—sometimes all of them. Then they don't have seeds to plant. When you receive resources, ask God which ones are for planting and which ones are for consuming. Don't eat your seed. Plant it for a hundredfold harvest.

BUILDING YOUR PROSPEROUS SOCIAL LIFE

How can you sow into your community to make it a better place? What is it that God has given you that you can provide? How might you socially widen your area of influence to sow into helping your community (and therefore yourself) prosper?

- If you are already sowing seeds, ask for wisdom and strategy to be increasingly growing in the sowing you do.
- Are you only sowing into a church community? Or are you also modeling your giving after God, who gave freely to all, and sowing into the community in general?

- Ask God to show you what you can expect to reap from sowing. Be intentional. It is not healthy for a farmer to sow and then not make a plan to reap. Sowing and reaping have to be equally as intentional, or a whole crop can go to waste.
- What do you want to reap? A better place for your children to grow up, less crime, more resources?

PROSPERITY PRAYER

God, I thank You for Your love and faithfulness to sow into us. You are a great God to make so many investments in us. Thank You that we have a process in You to thrive in. We can jump right into the abundance of You in the slow time-release process of sowing. It will keep our hearts pure toward You and connected to Your ways. Thank You that we can learn sowing from our ultimate farmer, Jesus. You always loved being in the gardens.

CREATING HOLISTIC PROSPERITY

 Relationships and Family: Plant positive interactions. Aim to plan ten positive interactions with family members for every one negative interaction. Pray the negative interactions do not produce lasting fruit of resentment, bitterness, and anger.

 Spiritual: Take the gifts God has given you—spiritual discernment, helps, hospitality, teaching—and sow weekly into your gifts to make them stronger.

Health: Be cautious to notice when emotional reactions of stress, anger, and disappointment are seeds that you are planting in your life. Make sure to pull them up and not let them take root and grow to overtake your emotional garden with thorns and thistles.

 Financial: Sow into investments that will increase your finances—for example: buying in bulk, buying an espresso machine instead of going out for coffee, buying a meal kit instead of going out to eat.

 Professional: Sow into your natural skill sets through education and mentoring (formal or informal is fine); the internet can be a huge source of education and mentoring.

 Mindset: Sowing into a sound mind allows you to reap a sound life. Peace in your mind is a skill to sow, protect, and cultivate to produce a crop of healthy mindsets.

49

Favor with God

May the favor of the Lord our God rest
on us;
establish the work of our hands for us—
yes, establish the work of our hands.
—PSALM 90:17 NIV

We previously discussed favor with man, but when building a prosperous life, it is important to also consider favor with God. Jesus grew in favor with God while He was on earth. This is perplexing to some. How could the beloved Son of God grow and increase His favor with His Father? Through relationship! Presumably, this is just as any other child might increase their favor with their parents through obedience, trustworthy behavior, kindness, time together, and more.

Jesus did not just take the favor of God and keep it to Himself. He took the favor He had with God and distributed it for a prosperous journey for friends and family and community. Favor with God can be pulled from a spiritual realm and extend into our social sphere. Moses had favor in the eyes of the Lord to walk out and bestow statutes of the Lord to his community. He incorporated that favor to the people he was leading.

God also gives favor to whole groups based on the actions of one. For example, in the Bible His favor was given to the Israelites. They received upgrades simply because they were part of the offspring and community. People like Ruth, who were not Israelites, gained favor through marriage and joining the people of Israel. God provides favor for social causes, churches, and social influence. Leaders have favor with God in a church, which impacts the congregation.

Both of us have spent seasons of our lives in hidden places with God. For me (Ally), I spent about two years devoting a large part of my free time in a prayer room—simply resting in the presence of God. During this time, I developed a deep intimacy with God, and out of this place I believe I received favor with God. It is not that I earned favor, because favor can't be earned. But during this time God revealed open doors and an awareness of things that others might even walk past because we can only see them through relational intimacy. I believe that I continue to live from a place of fruitfulness because God delights in me, and this belief helps me to look for ways God has and will favor me in the future.

Part of the favor also comes as I seek God and partner with Him, He establishes me in the work He has given me to do. For example, I have been fortunate to receive almost every job and doctoral training program I really wanted. This is more than good luck. It is the act of listening to God and what He has for me, partnering with that, and aligning my heart with the goal. God opened doors for me to receive and achieve what I wanted, because I believe it was what He wanted too. The work I do deeply impacts the community I live in. Through teaching, empowering, and supporting, any favor I receive is passed on to the community of people I work for and with.

When we are postured before the face of God, we will shine with the brightness of His rising. His favor will begin to exude from us and around us. Our lives will change for the better in every way imaginable. Doors of impossibility will open because God opened them. Chains of opposition will be broken because God broke them. The favor of God can become your best friend. Invite His favor into all your social spheres and see what God can do. Test Him on this. He will prove Himself faithful.

BUILDING YOUR PROSPEROUS SOCIAL LIFE

Jesus' life shows us that we can increase in favor with God. Start today by trying one of the following:

- Spend time in prayer and meditation simply becoming aware that God wants you to increase in favor with Him.
- Ask Him what favor with Him would look like for you.
- Consider and receive the favor God wants to give you.
- Pursue God's thoughts, heart, and mind to help you understand where His favor is and how to align with it.

PROSPERITY PRAYER

Your favor is the most highly coveted gift in the world. To be favored by the God who created all and has all power is humbling and awe inspiring. Help us to use the favor You have given to rightly serve others and You, just as Jesus did. Help us remain aware that all the favor we have in this world started with and in You.

CREATING HOLISTIC PROSPERITY

 Relationships and Family: Our families can open up doors of favor with God, and we can open up doors of favor for our families. It is an upgrade by proximity through their experiences, walk, and perspectives.

 Spiritual: We can choose to actively pursue favor with God. If Jesus grew in favor with God, we see that through obedience we, too, can gain more favor.

 Health: God bestows favor through healing. God will begin to abound in breakthroughs, giftings, and miracles with someone who has found favor in His eyes.

 Financial: Those who have favor with God will receive financial breakthroughs and surprises.

 Professional: God will give provision to those He favors to be at the right place at the right time to receive honor, promotion, increased responsibilities, increased ability to help others, and so forth. Joseph and Esther are two examples of this.

 Mindset: Believing we are favored by God will cause us to look at the possible upgrade in each situation and to walk in a way that causes others to see us as favored.

Conclusion

Keep this Book of the Law always on your lips;
meditate on it day and night, so that you may be
careful to do everything written in it. Then you
will be prosperous and successful.

—JOSHUA 1:8 NIV

What an amazing journey! From Adam and Eve in the garden of Eden, to the disciples pulling in 153 fish from the Sea of Galilee, to you in the present moment and place in time, God has provided. His eternal desire is that you would be brought into the fullness of His prosperity. This is God's heart for you. This is His plan for you, which has been hidden in His Word through the centuries, providing ways for you to prosper. His provision is limitless. It will never run out.

Through this book we hope you have come to consider how prosperity is not money at all. *God is prosperity.* Jesus is the way, the truth, and the life. He wants you to know and partner with Him. Partner with Him and steward and care for the revelation He gives you through His Word. Take these tools you have been given and incorporate them into your life. Fully embrace the prosperity He brings.

In this book we have examined forty-nine ways of prosperity. We have seen how they relate to seven areas of life and discovered the width and depth of how prosperity may be applied holistically to your life. Prosperity is a lifelong journey. It bubbles forth out of consistency and persistence and a willingness to learn. We are excited to have had you on this part of the journey with us and invite you to continue and find ways to implement these principles in your life! If you are excited to continue this journey, you can find more on our website or listen to our free podcast, *Radiant Thoughts*, on the ways of prosperity. We are on a journey, incorporating these amazing behaviors, mindsets, and facets of God into our daily lives.

God is with us on this journey of becoming more fruitful and prosperous. Even more, we would say that God *is* the journey! Through the ways of prosperity, we have come to know and love Him more. We have understood Him more. In Him is the only way to all true prosperity.

We encourage you to not keep this journey to yourself. Invite your friends, families, churches, and communities. All things are possible with God, and He is on your side. We are cheering you on along the way. We hope this will be the most prosperous year of your life. We hope you can connect with the prosperity of the Father and invite Him more into your world every day.

"And whatever you do, whether in word or deed, do it all in the name of the Lord Jesus, giving thanks to God the Father through him" (Colossians 3:17 NIV).

BUILDING YOUR PROSPEROUS LIFE

Over the preceding chapters we have explored how forty-nine ways of prosperity apply to seven areas of life. We want to take a moment to reflect and ask the following questions.

- Which avenue of life do you prosper in the most? How can you share that?
- Which avenue of life do you struggle in the most? What is one thing you will take away to improve that?
- Which way of prosperity surprised you the most?
- Which way of prosperity do you feel you are starting to master?
- Who do you know who would benefit from an invitation to the journey of greater prosperity?

PROSPERITY PRAYER

You, Jesus, are our way of prosperity. Thank You for always being there for us. We look to You as we fashion our next steps in this journey of life. Thank You for Your abounding love and direction. Your support is unwavering. Lead us and guide us in Your ways. Make us objects of Your love today. Bless You, Jesus.

CREATING HOLISTIC PROSPERITY

Now it is your turn! Whatever we have received, we are called to give away. Reflect on what you have learned so far, and think about how you can impact others going forward.

 Relationships and Family: Who can you share this message with among your family and close friends? How would you like to see them impacted?

Spiritual: How have you been spiritually empowered by this message? Who can you share that with? How can this help your spiritual family?

 Health: What is an aspect of emotional or physical health you have learned that you can consider sharing with others?

 Financial: What financial strategy can you share with others?

 Professional: Who in your professional community might be empowered by something you have learned in this book?

 Mindset: What mindset can you adopt to help you better serve the needs and lives of others?

 Social: How could your community be enhanced by what you have learned?

Acknowledgments

This book would not have been possible without the support, encouragement and mentoring we have gained from so many throughout our lives.

I (Ally) would like to express my tremendous gratitude to my grandparents Bill and Betty for being models who have demonstrated so many ways of prosperity to me. Thank you for spending your lives opening up so many doors of opportunity and prosperity to me and others. Your love is, and will always be, a beacon of light in my life.

I (Jeremy) would like to thank Pastor Bill Johnson and Kris Vallotton for making a way for me and so many others to learn about how big God is. Your contribution to my life echoes each and every day.

We are grateful for all those, seen and unseen, who have sacrificed time, energy, and resources helping us, and others, to prosper in life.

Notes

1. Steve Schultz, "Pray, Pursue God . . . and *Laugh* While You Do It," The Elijah List, May 8, 2009, https://www.elijahlist.com/words /display_word.html?ID=7613.
2. Gary Chapman, *The 5 Love Languages* (Northfield Publishing, 2015).
3. *Cambridge English Dictionary*, s.v. "ingenuity," https://dictionary .cambridge.org/us/dictionary/english/ingenuity.
4. *Perfect Bid: The Contestant Who Knew Too Much*, directed by C. J. Wallis, documentary featuring Ted Slauson (El Segundo, CA: Gravitas Ventures, 2017).

About the Authors

JEREMY BUTROUS

After graduating from Bethel School of Ministry, Jeremy has been working with ministers, speakers, and churches for the last decade. He has had the privilege to work with both for profits and nonprofits, supporting their product development and strategic growth. In addition to his work in ministry, he enjoys investing and is currently part owner of a small investing company. He has a passion for writing, and he has authored several other books, including *Praying Through the Seven Mountains* and *Transcending Mindsets*.

ALLY BUTROUS

Ally started college at age fifteen, and soon realized the only path she felt called to was a career where she could help, empower, and inspire others to live their best lives. She has since completed two master's degrees in psychology (Rosemead School of Psychology at Biola University and Pepperdine University). She will receive her doctorate in psychology in September 2020. Ally has experience providing mental health services in a variety of settings, including treatment centers for children and teens, university and church counseling centers, and a hospital's psychiatric department. She also enjoys teaching, speaking, and writing as means to communicate a powerful balance of spiritual and practical wisdom.

JEREMY AND ALLY

When Jeremy and Ally met, they knew their relationship was one of love, mutual admiration, and also powerful collaborative purposes. In 2018 they started a consulting business together, working to help grow the audience, products, and online presence of Christian authors and speakers. Between them, they have ghostwritten fourteen manuscripts for Christian authors. In their free time, Jeremy and Ally love to connect with family, travel the world, and explore the restaurants in Los Angeles, where they live with their bichon-poodle, Pepper.